COMPANY

COMPANY

A Chosen Life

John Montague

Duckworth

First published in 2001 by
Gerald Duckworth & Co. Ltd
61 Frith Street, London W1D 3JL
Tel: 020 7434 4242
Fax: 020 7434 4420
Email: enquiries@duckworth-publishers.co.uk
www.ducknet.co.uk

© 2001 by John Montague

All rights reserved. No part of this publication
may be reproduced, stored in a retrieval system, or
transmitted, in any form or by any means, electronic,
mechanical, photocopying, recording or otherwise,
without the prior permission of the publisher.

The right of John Montague to be identified as the Author of
the Work has been asserted by him in accordance with
the Copyright, Designs and Patents Act 1988.

The publishers gratefully acknowledge permission to reproduce the
photographs listed below: (John Montague) © Brendan Somerville;
(Brendan Behan) © Hulton Archive; (Thomas Kinsella, John Montague,
Liam Miller) by Henri Cartier-Bresson; (William Butler Yeats, his wife George)
© Hulton Archive (Norman MacCaig) © Claddagh Records; (Tom Kinsella
on the ramparts) by Jeffrey Craig © Claddagh Records; (Red Hugh) © Irish
Press; (John Montague, Samuel Beckett) © Patrick Monaghan (Seamus Heaney)
© Claddagh Records. All other photographs are taken from
the author's private collection.

Every effort has been made to obtain permission to use copyright
materials; the publishers trust that their apologies will be accepted
for any errors or omissions.

A catalogue record for this book is available
from the British Library

ISBN 0 7156 3016 4

Typeset by Ray Davies
Printed in Great Britain by
Bookcraft (Bath) Ltd, Midsomer Norton, Avon

Acknowledgements

Thanks to Sarah Such, my brilliant and tireless editor, and to Tom for his initial support. Two chapters, on Mrs Yeats, and my visit to her with Theodore Roethke, have appeared in *The Southern Review*. Part of the Behan chapter appeared in the *Sunday Tribune* (Dublin) and 'Scylla and Charybdis' in the Poetry Ireland publication: *Watching the River Flow*.

Lines from the play 'The Countess Cathleen' and the poem 'A Vision' by W.B. Yeats reproduced by permission of A.P. Watt Ltd on behalf of Michael B. Yeats.

Lines from Patrick Kavanagh's 'Prelude' are reprinted with the permission of the Estate of the late Katharine B. Kavanagh, through the Jonathan Williams Literary Agency.

Lines from 'September Elegy' by Tom Parkinson taken from *Collected Poems* by kind permission of Ariel Parkinson and the Estate.

Extract from 'From the Notebook of a European Tramp' taken from *Michael Hamburger: Collected Poems 1941–1994*, published by Anvil Press Poetry in 1995.

Lines from 'The Loss of Strength' in *Too Great a Vine* (Bridge Press 1995, Dolmen Press 1957), and from 'Beyond the Pale' in *Flight to Africa* (Dolmen Press 1963) reproduced by permission of R. Dardis Clarke, 21 Pleasants Street, Dublin 8, Ireland.

Lines from 'Baggot Street Deserta' by Tom Kinsella reproduced by kind permission of Carcanet.

Lines from 'My Little Red Knife' by Patrick Galvin reproduced by permission of the author c/o Cork University Press.

Lines from 'Herbert Street Revisited', 'The Siege of Mullingar', 'A Chosen Light', Salute in Passing', 'All Legendary Obstacles', 'Soliloquy on a Southern Strand', 'A Charm' and 'Coatlicue' taken from *Collected Poems* and from 'Claddagh Raga' taken from *Smashing the Piano* by John Montague reproduced by kind permission of the author and Gallery Press, 1995.

Lines from *Borstal Boy* by Brendan Behan published by Hutchinson. Used by permission of the Random House Group Ltd.

Poems by Theodore Roethke taken from the *Collected Poems*, published by Faber and Faber Ltd (UK) and Doubleday (US) reproduced by kind permission of the publishers and Beatrice Roethke, Theodore Roethke Estate.

Lines from 'In Memory of W.B. Yeats' by W.H. Auden taken from *Collected Poems* reproduced by permission of Faber and Faber Ltd.

Lines from *Piedra del Sol* taken from the *Collected Poems* by Octavio Paz reproduced by kind permission of New Directions, Mexico City.

Line from 'America' and eight lines from 'Howl' in ALLEN GINSBERG: SELECTED POEMS 1947-1995 (Penguin Books 1997, first published in <u>Howl, Before and After</u>: *San Francisco Bay Area (1955-1956)*) © Allen Ginsberg 1996 reproduced by permission.

Lines from 'Riprap', included in *A Range of Poems* by Gary Snyder, Fulcrum Press.

Lines from 'The Shark's Parlour' and 'Cherry Log Road' by James Dickey (*Buckdancer's Choice,* 1965) reproduced by permission of his widow and Wesleyan University Press.

Preface

A Chosen Life is the first part of a memoir and, like memory itself, it weaves in and out of chronology. But be patient and, hopefully, all or nearly all will be revealed. I have assumed a certain familiarity with the streets of Dublin, Paris and the Bay Area in those hopeful days of the 1960s.

For Elizabeth, without whom…
and the ghost of Thomas Parkinson

Contents

Prologue	Mrs Yeats: Practical Mystic	11
Chapter One	Dublin, Underground	21
Chapter Two	Scylla and Charybdis	35
Chapter Three	As Good as a Play, or, A Human Behan	43
Chapter Four	Liam Dolmen, or Hell on a Green Isle	71
Chapter Five	Claddagh Raga	89
Chapter Six	A Chosen Life	101
Chapter Seven	Samuel Beckett, Neighbour	123
Chapter Eight	Dance On, Dance On, or A Rose for George	153
Chapter Nine	Passage to California	171

PROLOGUE

MRS YEATS: PRACTICAL MYSTIC

I came to know Mrs Yeats through Tom Parkinson, the Californian poet and critic, when he was working on the Yeats manuscripts in the mid-1950s. I think I actually guided him to her Palmerston Road house when he went there for the first time; those quiet, shaded avenues were familiar to me from my student days in Dublin, when I had passed through on my way to the Carnegie library in Rathmines.

During those dreamy years of reading and writing, and wandering the Dublin streets, I had already begun to get used to the idea of poets as living creatures. I would glimpse Padraic Colum, whose poems I had read at school, coming and going from his sister's house, which was almost next door to my digs in Beechwood Avenue. He was as regular as the swallows because he and his wife migrated back from America every spring. He seemed a friendly man, sharp-eyed and smiling, indeed almost like an alert little bird himself. His soft voice still held the cadence of the Irish midlands as he recited or spoke of poetry. But neither he nor anyone else I met in those early days told me that the widow of our greatest poet lived just round the corner.

Padraic Colum was gentle and approachable, whereas Mrs Yeats seemed daunting, to judge from Tom Parkinson's comments. He was very fond of her, but said she was one of the most quick-witted women he had ever met, intolerant of all pretension. I finally got caught into meeting her when they were having tea in the lounge of the Shelbourne Hotel. And worse still, Parkinson introduced me by saying that I was by way of being a poet. 'God help him,' was her first comment, and I thought that was it, short and sharp, when she made room for me beside her in a most friendly way, declaring that she had seen some of my poetry, always the way to a young poet's heart. Soon we were gossiping, thick as thieves, and as far as I remember, the tea was followed by something a little stronger.

I found George Yeats entrancing, a marvellous blend of English and grafted Irish, a mixture I was not to meet again until I met Joan Hague, Eric Gill's daughter. Parkinson had not prepared me for George's extraordinary sense of humour; there is a certain sort of brisk, no nonsense approach which is supposed to be characteristically English, and which often sounds rude to Irish ears, but she had honed it to a note of gentle repartee. She used it to make fun of herself and others, to carve through the Celtic Twilight; although she had become part of literary Dublin through her husband, she maintained an ironical distance. (A distance which I gather she had cultivated early, as a young English lady suddenly at the mercy of Dublin gossip.) She clearly found being a poet's widow only a cut above being an unpaid museum keeper, and obsequious scholars earned her private wrath.

'Why, they don't even take a drink! And they ask me to read his handwriting. Nobody could. He couldn't. And then they hint about love letters, and how I felt about Maud Gonne.'

Her views on that subject were more than lively, and I wondered if their paths still sometimes crossed, since Maud Gonne lived only a short distance away in the same area of South Dublin. But Mrs Yeats was not one for the high style, despite the formidable personality of her husband, and the airs and graces of Yeats's early muse would not have been to her taste, despite their common English background. Indeed, most of the ladies of her time in Dublin were not greatly taken with Maud Gonne, whom they accused of coveting the limelight, especially where the attentions of gentlemen were concerned. In theatrical terms, she was regarded as a great upstager, and the Dublin of the period, where literary and political personalities intersected so often, provided many opportunities for her kind of high drama. Ever since Yeats cast her in the leading role of Cathleen ni Houlihan, she seemed to regard herself as the embodiment of Ireland: a brave, though suffering, beauty.

Actually, I had met Maud Gonne as well, introduced by my writer pal John Jordan, who admired her lofty, almost camp style, and her surprisingly upper middle class English accent. But I found her too self conscious, too aware of her role in Irish history and letters: 'All the Olympians.' The marvellously tall, straight-backed Pallas Athene of those early photographs, with square jaw and level eyes, had been reduced by time to a hooped, frail figure, scarfed in cigarette smoke. In fact, she reminded me of no one so much as the old pensioners of my early childhood, hobbling down to Garvaghey post office in their dusty Edwardian finery. But her frailty did not seem to me to diminish her dreamy arrogance, as she lived again her glory days. I suppose I was a bit intimidated by her.

Whereas I was so taken with Mrs Yeats that I took to calling on her on my own whenever I was in the area, and always came away bubbling with stories. Contrary to what one might have expected, she was not mean about other Irish writers, except one or two who had offended Willy, but profoundly curious about their progress. 'All right,' she'd say, 'he's not bad but he's not doing enough.' She was a great believer in getting down to it and not being self satisfied, not wasting one's own or other people's time. I defended Austin Clarke to her and she accepted that his middle work was much better than his early. 'Willy was probably wrong about him. But what about those dreary reviews in the *Irish Times*? Why doesn't he get his wife to write them, she couldn't sound worse? Or the dog? Someone should give him money to do what he wants to do before he's past it.'

Indeed, Austin was to come into his own, returning to poetry after a gap of seventeen years. But did he 'woo too late with open arms'? She was harder on Patrick Kavanagh, our other senior poet. 'The rubbish that man talks. Being rude is important only at the right time, otherwise no one listens to you. He abuses other people as a way of not writing himself. Perhaps someone ought to give him some money, as well, and shut him up and get him to sit down and work. At least he's lively,' she added, and darted a quick smirk over the sherry glass, 'unlike your Austin Clarke. Maybe if we gave Kavanagh all those tiresome books to review, that would dampen him down a bit, and then send the other one into the public houses to get a bit squiffy.'

Her recipe for creativity seemed to be to create a bit of a stir, but she was also kind. When we had discussed someone, she would insist that I should give her respects, if and when I met them, especially their wives, if they were matrimonially equipped. She was acutely conscious of the position of Nora Clarke, still not legally Austin's wife, though she was the mother of his children. But with that sympathy went a curious injunction which came back again and again, as refrain. 'They're not working enough. It's up to you young people to put a bomb under them. That's what they want, something to wake them all up. Willy always liked a good row.'

She meant it metaphorically, of course. With a dignified mournfulness, the always courteous Clarke tried to maintain the tradition of the literary salon while the roar from the pubs grew louder. His Sunday soirées at Bridge House were a last vestige of Dublin's old literary life, and I couldn't see myself calling on him and greeting him with the fiery salutations of Mrs Yeats. After all, Austin was trying to keep alive the now guttering flame of the Irish Literary Revival that her husband had helped to kindle. But when I read Nancy Mitford or Evelyn Waugh I seem to hear the voice of Mrs Yeats, with a few sherries under her belt, urging me to put a bomb under the tail of some senior Irish poet. The only thing that earned her unreserved scorn was not working. I mentioned a poet who seemed to me to write well but had never published a book.

'So the poor little acorn waited to be an oak,' she said impatiently. 'You know, John, that anyone can get a poem into a paper now and then, but that's only a start, and don't you forget it. A poet has no right not to write,' a sentiment echoed to me by her friend, the poet Kathleen Raine, years later.

Our relationship became more firmly founded when, in the office of the Irish Tourist Board, where I worked, I unearthed a little known photograph of Yeats – little known because it was neither formal nor formidable – a private not a public image. It showed the slippered poet resting in an armchair, smiling with vague benevolence at the world, his sheepdog at his feet. It turned out to be Mrs Yeats's favourite picture of the great man she called Willy, and she gazed at it with deep fondness. 'It's hard to know who is more long suffering, the poet or the dog. Probably all the visitors had just left, and he could relax.'

Her tone was protective, indulgent, a wife speaking about her husband, not a curator extolling a public monument. Even motherly, although she was half his age: one must remember that in addition to being the companion, and equal, of a very great poet, Mrs Yeats was a mother, and I think I benefited from that as well as her real interest in poetry. Yeats was in his mid-fifties when they married, and already set in his grand ways, more used to being taken care of by Lady Gregory and other ministering angels than to the insistent demands of fatherhood. Can one imagine W.B. proudly wheeling a pram, or spreadeagled on the nursery floor with teddy bears and dolls? Anne Yeats has an endearing story about travelling home on the bus behind her oblivious father, probably returning distracted from a film. (He was a Wild West and Detective fan, anything to cool the engine.)

So George Yeats took care of the children as well as looking after the great man; and when he died, she became what would now be called a single parent, holding her little family together. While not buttressed by an organised faith, like the black garbed Catholic matrons of my youth, she was sustained by an ideal of service. I can only imagine the atmosphere she created around them at Riversdale, but if she was a mystic, she was a practical one. And if, as Yeats believed, the poet should be lucky, then he certainly was in his choice of wife, despite his many hesitations. Of medium height and swart complexion, George Yeats did not have the grand style of Maud Gonne, but her vivacity was immediately compelling, and she knew how to cherish those in her care.

I now regret that I was so deferential, and, for me, polite, as I had been taught to be with older people. An ignorant young man of Ulster Catholic background, I did not have the equipment to really profit from the acquaintance of this marvellous woman, on either the poetic or spiritual level. When I browsed through Yeats's library, I was impressed by the number of books on history and philosophy, but I had yet to read *A Vision*, his *summa mystica*. And when I was gazing with bemused perplexity at the elaborate diagrams in the astrological and mystical notebooks, and wondering about their connection with poetry, I had only to consult the oracle in the next room. Brendan Behan was fond of quoting the dying Gertrude Stein as saying, 'What is the answer?' Then, sighing, 'What is the question?' I did not yet know the question so I could not ask for the answer. All I knew was that there was something in Mrs Yeats's company that made me feel at ease babbling about my poetic plans, those early poems which would appear in *Forms of Exile* and *Poisoned Lands*. They did not have the plangency and music of her husband's work, which now rang over our heads like a deep, solemn bell, an arching cathedral of sound and sense, but she seemed to feel that my scribbles were somehow worthwhile, and gave her gruff benediction.

What still stays with me is the memory of a warm, loving woman, with a capacity for total, uncomplaining devotion to the tasks at hand, private and public. She loved her Willy, and revered his genius, and while, from a feminist point of view, she may seem to have lived a subordinate life, she clearly did not see it that way. She had been his companion in one of the great visionary adventures of our time. Many of the late poems were dictated through her, as he acknowledges in 'The Gift of Haroun el Rashid'. A dusky lass, she was Sheba to his Solomon, a noble lady equal to the philosopher-poet, fit consort for a king, to use the old phrase. 'Speaking in divers tongues', she had been the psychic conduit for his greatest work, *The Tower* and *The Winding Stair*. And as an initiate herself, she was Yeats's equal in rank in the Order of the Golden Dawn, using her talents as a medium to see off the double-pronged Gonne threat. (It seems obvious that neither Maud nor her daughter Iseult really wished to bed Yeats, but they liked having their pet poet around.

And as an earnest young poet, Yeats had impaled himself on an old-fashioned courtly love ideal – an ideal from which Mrs Yeats rescued him.)

So George's share in *A Vision* is one of the great matrimonial strokes of history, giving the weary lover and poet back his own unconscious as a *schema* of belief:

> All those gyres and cubes and midnight things
> Are but a new expression of her body
> Drunk with the bitter sweetness of her youth.
> And now my utmost mystery is out.

While John Jordan would always urge me to come back with him to see Maud Gonne again, I had very little desire to do so. John assured me that she, too, could be great craic, but the old lady in black I saw toiling through the Dublin streets was a daunting spectacle, as if she had come to embody the vision of the hag at the beginning of *Cathleen ni Houlihan*, a part she had famously played. For me, Maud Gonne was a subject of poetry: Mrs Yeats was a source.

(Which is not to say that Yeats's love for Maud Gonne was not fruitful. But to some degree it was a love without particularity. Because he did not really live with her, his love for her could leave the boundaries of his self undisturbed, while Mrs Yeats taught him love in the dailiness of life.)

And she is still a source, for me. In dreams, she reappears, generous and smiling. The nose and cheeks are a bit more red, not only because she liked a tipple, but because she has always had a high, bright complexion. She looks like a doll, with her round, lively eyes like two shiny black buttons. In one dream, I'm hurrying along a Dublin road in the rain, my raincoat collar flaring, but without an umbrella. Mrs Yeats is standing at a bus stop under an ample black umbrella. 'Take this, John,' she says, proffering it to me, 'I have another at home.' Meaning, I think, the old boy, her husband, whom George Moore once wickedly compared to an umbrella left behind at a picnic.

In another dream, I am alone with her again, in that mysterious library, and she presents me with a thick, dull gold ring with a curious bright aura. 'You should have something of his, to remember him by.' The ring feels heavy, a responsibility but not an oppressive one.

'Remember what I've always told you,' she continues. 'You must work on. Forget about fame, envy, and competition. They never really worried him, except as provocation. You must sing on, indifferent as a dormouse or a willow wren. The song will be heard.' I feel suddenly light-hearted, as though the ring represents some kind of completion. Finally, I have asked the question, and got the answer.

CHAPTER ONE

DUBLIN, UNDERGROUND

In autumn, 1954, against the unlikely background of Iowa, I met a titled young Frenchwoman with an eager grin and golden-brown eyes, called Madeleine de Brauer. We had both gone there as visiting scholars, and soon moved into a small wooden house together, something quite unusual in the Grant Wood American Middle West of that time. I think we got a kind of fool's pardon as eccentric, sex-mad foreigners in those repressed Eisenhower years, when couples danced slowly in the Students' Union, cheek to cheek or her head on his shoulder, bodies pressed together in a tumid dream. Even my Poetry Workshop pal, Robert Bly, was puzzled. 'Why, John,' he asked, 'whenever I call you on the phone, does a woman's voice answer?'

Then our academic paths bifurcated, when she went to the French department at Champagne-Urbana, and I moved west to Berkeley, where I became a graduate teaching assistant to Tom Parkinson. We criss-crossed the western United States to meet each other, at D. H. Lawrence's Taos, and dipped down into Mexico for a long, hot summer. Soon we began to recognise that we had better get married, to remain longer together, to continue our conversation, and what the old Irish called 'the conversation of bodies', from which children might come. Indeed, in keeping with my rural

CHAPTER ONE

background, my deliberately unromantic proposal was 'Should we take out a breeding licence?'

So after a ceremony in Madeleine's family chapel in Normandy, we found ourselves in a lovely melancholy Georgian street in Dublin, near Baggot Street Bridge, and strategically close to where I worked at the Irish Tourist Office, Bord Failte, in Mount Street Crescent. We had a basement flat in 6, Herbert Street, with one large room where we ate, read, worked and slept. Although the space was constrained, it was charming, and we did not have to battle the Great American Cockroach, as in our sweltering Iowa billet. In fact, the pattern of concentrating life's essentials – work, meals, bed – in one small area has repeated itself often in my life. And beside the bathroom there was a small back bedroom which, when children did not arrive, slowly became a haven for several, indeed for many, couples, undeterred in their fervour by the narrowness of the room, indeed relishing the privacy of this discreet nest. For sex had not yet reared its beautiful siren head in De Valera's Ireland, either, where we lived under a regime as oppressive as puritan America.

But this pattern of sheltering erotic exiles took a while to establish; at first we had mainly bachelor visitors. Clancy Sigal was a stray pal from Los Angeles, where he had been a scriptwriter and journalist, on the edge of Hollywood. Disaffected with McCarthy's America, he was establishing a new reputation in England, with his 'Youth' reportage in the *Observer*, and his Orwellian study, *Week-End in Dinlock*, set in a depressed mining town. He liked Dublin, and especially Brendan Behan, our next-door neighbour, since he felt they shared the same socialist views and were both working-class writers, like his favourite Americans, Harvey Swados and Nelson Algren, inheritors of the American Leftist dream.

Clancy took to our Dublin scene like a duck to water; although he did not always understand what was going on in late-night drinking establishments like the Piper's Club or a cobwebby eighteenth-century shebeen like the Brazen Head, he found it refreshingly informal after literary London. So much so, that he decided to return to us with his companion, a novelist called Doris Lessing. But first he sent us Algren, who was a pure delight, an old-fashioned American eccentric with a winking electric tie, and a wacky sense of humour to match it. He has left an account of his visit in his book, *Who Lost an American*, which gives a good description of the still repressed and gloomy Dublin of the late 1950s, gulls creaking over the sleepy streets, with their Guinness dray horses and clouds of dark-clothed cyclists. But he recounts a hilarious brush with the poet Kavanagh, which I will describe anon. And Nelson was even happier with Behan, who had prepared for his visit by reading all his available work, especially *A Walk on the Wild Side*, its picture of life in the New Orleans brothel quarter bound to appeal to the author of *The Hostage*.

'Compliments pass when the Quality meet' was one of Brendan's mottoes, and the two happily exchanged comments and quotations, as we travelled from pub to pub in the Dublin foothills, with a taxi driver from the North Side who bawled out songs with Brendan. And we ended up the evening in a pub with various relatives of Brendan who had been transported from North Side slums to bleak housing estates, including an aunt who was so drunk that she lost one of her boots. Later, a long-suffering Madeleine came to succour and feed Algren and myself, recalling Patrick Kavanagh's lines from 'Prelude':

> Count then your blessings, hold in mind
> All that has loved you or been kind:

CHAPTER ONE

> Those women on their mercy missions,
> Rescue work with kiss or kitchens...

Determined to show Algren that Dublin could rival the stews of Chicago, Madeleine and I would take him to an extraordinary establishment called Anne's Tea Shop, a shabby little restaurant in decorous Nassau Street, which was transmogrified after closing time into a class of night club, with something stronger in the teacups. Cracked records played as people lurched on to the small dance floor. Like Dolly Fawcett's in an older Dublin, or Katie Barry's in Cork, it was an Irish solution to an Irish problem. And with its surreptitious cups of after-hours whiskey, it was probably like my uncle's speakeasy in Prohibition Brooklyn. But our carousing didn't last long, and Nelson was delighted when the joint was raided by grinning *gardai*, and his name and address were ritually noted, as well as that of the young Dublin girl on his knee, who was hoping to get to America.

*

Nelson and Clancy's enthusiastic reports had convinced Doris Lessing to visit Dublin. We picked her and Clancy up at the airport, in our ancient Austin motorcar, and showed them the sights, the curve of Killiney Bay, the monastic city of Glendalough, the Hill of Howth where Molly Bloom said 'yes'. We lay in the grass, and when Madeleine plaited a flower chain and placed it across my loin, Doris was impressed, comparing it to that famous scene from *Lady Chatterley's Lover*.

Doris was definitely not a pub person, so I brought her round to see Mervyn Wall, who worked as Secretary in the Arts Council, because she had read his wry account of contemporary Ireland in his novel *Leaves for the Burning*. Mervyn was crouched in a corner, surrounded by fashionable abstract paintings bought by Father O'Sullivan, the Jesuit director of the Arts Council, paintings that the besieged Mervyn clearly found chill and inhuman. Doris was amused by his resemblance to a Dickensian clerk, crabbed, long-suffering yet cargoed with self-protective gossip about his superiors. (But probably even Mervyn's mordant imagination could not have conceived of a time when his Reverend Director, Father O'Sullivan, would be accused of sharing a mistress with Graham Greene.)

Most of the meals were taken over by intense literary and ideological discussion, which Madeleine, who did the cooking, found wearing. She felt that you always had to justify yourself politically with Doris, a process that had to be re-run the next day, in case you had defected overnight. One evening, over the dinner table, Madeleine launched into an impassioned analysis of her family, and the dismaying social irrelevance of her whole French upper class background. They were briefly sympathetic, but the next day Doris seemed to have forgotten it, as once more she and Clancy engaged in their endless dialectic, like earnest students in a leftist café. It seemed to be their kind of love talk.

I think that is why Doris fell foul of Brendan. We had all been at Stratford East for the opening night of Brendan's play, *The Hostage*, in October 1958, where Brendan made a witty curtain-call speech. She was also an admirer of *The Quare Fellow*, his passionate drama about a prison execution, which she had seen in London, and of which she approved politically because the hanging debate was, so to speak, in the air.

And then there was the class issue. While Doris herself was a middle class intellectual, she would have had to admit Brendan's

CHAPTER ONE

superior socialist credentials. Claude Cockburn once ironically commented that you had to be either absolutely top-drawer (like, presumably, himself, and Madeleine) or totally bottom-shelf, and Brendan's qualifications in the second department could not be bettered. Clancy, for example, had stories about going to school wearing cardboard boxes for shoes, but he recognised Brendan's unassailable claim to be the lowest of the low, part of the International Proletariat, with his mother defiantly singing *The Red Flag* even in the Shelbourne Hotel.

For the 1920s' Dublin Brendan grew up in had once been part of the international workers' movement; Marx, after all, had thought the Revolution more likely to come in Ireland than Russia, and the lengthy 1913 strike had more effect on the working class of Dublin than the purely national uprising of 1916. We brought Doris and Clancy to see James Plunkett's dramatisation of the 1913 strike, *The Risen People*, in the Abbey Theatre, but they thought it was old-fashioned Agit. Propaganda, not realising how close it was still to the memories of many older Dubliners, including the Behan family.

It was, I think, on a Sunday morning that I brought Doris up to beard Brendan in his den. Alas, things very quickly went wrong, perhaps because he was in a foul humour, either still hungover from the night before, and/or he had been quarrelling with his wife Beatrice. Also, Doris' righteous earnestness, her assumption of comradeship, obviously annoyed Brendan, who could be difficult, indeed awful, jagged as a hedgehog. He reviled her as a 'professional black', 'a middle-class *New Statesman* Liberal' who 'didn't know the Real Working Class', which seemed to me another kind of reverse snobbery. And she didn't like him much either, the way he spoke to Beatrice, the untidiness and filth of the apartment with bottles and newspapers scattered everywhere. And the way he played to the gallery, a kind of histrionic Irish attitude she loathed. I had fallen foul of Brendan myself, so I sympathised with her tense cold anger at being taunted in this fashion. But on the other hand, she seemed uncomfortable with the Irish style of rough, teasing banter, being suspicious of the playful, and having an almost puritanical attitude towards 'the drink'.

Both Clancy and I were distressed by this confrontation, which I did think she took too seriously, Brendan being so obviously mercurial, a king on his own small throne, expressing his emotions as they arose. But I had noticed before that anything whimsical was frowned upon in her world, as though a sense of humour were a bourgeois weakness, and probably Irish as well: she did not take to Siobhan McKenna's somewhat boozy extravagance either. Although intelligent and attractive, Doris seemed embattled, prickly, full of theories about things, in a way like Mary McCarthy, whom I would meet in Berkeley some years later, though her expression was less harsh than Mary's scimitar smile. Perhaps their defensiveness was a style or an armour: it was harder then to be both a woman and a writer, wanting to be acknowledged for your achievement in a world where men still expected women to be decorative and demure. And certainly they were not expected to analyse their relationships with men in burning, confessional detail, as Madeleine's idol, Simone de Beauvoir, would her affair with Algren in both fiction and autobiography, to Nelson's disgust. A pattern Doris was about to follow, to Clancy's disgust as well.

My abiding memory of the visit of Doris Lessing to Herbert Street is of her sitting at the table in our big basement room, shuffling a series of school exercise books of various colours, and declaring that she was trying to write a different kind of novel, from varying points

CHAPTER ONE

of view; the names of some of the characters were already scrawled on the covers of the notebooks. She had the baffled look of a real artist embarking upon a real work of which she still knew very little, her new quest into the unknown. Would she be able to control her need to categorise, to place a rational template over experience? I believe I was glimpsing the slow coalescing of her multi-layered masterpiece, *The Golden Notebook*.

*

My own worst quarrel with Brendan was when I was speaking, perhaps boastfully, of my wife's family, a weakness I was prone to, being young and bedazzled by the amplitude of her Norman family tree as compared to my own few broken County Tyrone boughs. And indeed it was impressive: her great-great-grandfather, Maréchal d'Avoust, was the only noble among Napoleon's marshals, albeit a younger son, perhaps seeking advancement under the new regime. He was also a brilliant strategist, whose victory at Auerstaedt gained him a dukedom, although Tolstoy naturally does not give a flattering picture of him in *War and Peace*. 'Every time a d'Avoust is born,' says the family motto, 'a sword leaps from its scabbard'. And Madeleine's family was cluttered with generals, tall men with medals from myriad campaigns, her many uncles as well as her taciturn father, who had been commander of one of the few French tank regiments to face the Blitzkrieg. An event which had already changed her life, as well as mine, although we did not yet understand how.

'You shouldn't have told me that,' Brendan rebuked me almost wistfully, 'I was beginning to like the girl, and she's certainly too good for the likes of you. But it's not my France, and it shouldn't be yours. You should either be with the writers, or the ordinary working class, *les ouvriers*, who are the best company in Europe. Big and all as her family is, I bet there's no one who can sing a song, or tell a joke. Camus' mother was a washerwoman, and he played in goal in Algiers. The French Communist Party is the biggest in the West, and its poets, like Eluard and Aragon, are the people you should be associating with, not Dukes and Counts and all that right-wing reactionary brigade, who were probably on the wrong side during the Spanish Civil War. That's not the real France, or else it's the wrong half of it.'

And I remembered how, years before, when I was going to Paris, Brendan had given me two sets of addresses, one intellectual, and the other the *patron* of both a café and a *bordel*.

I walked away from him, and we did not speak for several weeks, which, since we both lived in Herbert Street, was not so easy. I tried to tell Madeleine about it, but she refused to understand, and said it was a storm in a pint glass, and that Brendan was perfectly entitled to dislike her family, as she often did herself. Nevertheless she was secretly proud of them, of the way her ancestor had protected the Jews of Hamburg, of how he waited with the Army of Paris, prepared to fight on after Waterloo, which might have been won if he had not been held back by Napoleon. And I had to say, as I got to know them better, that there was a fair scattering of eccentrics in her family, which had received this unknown Irishman with courtesy and kindness.

While Brendan was quick to anger, indeed sometimes over-ready for a scrap, he had no heart for a long-time feud, no appetite for the prolonged sulk, which almost came naturally to an Ulsterman like myself. As he himself has ruefully written, 'I suffer from a weakness of character that I can't keep up indignation for long.' So in Parsons

CHAPTER ONE

book shop on Baggot Street Bridge we would studiously avoid each other, with even Miss O'Flaherty, and certainly Miss King, giggling at our schoolboy petulance, and I couldn't risk going into any of my usual locals in case we found ourselves staring at each other – but it came to an abrupt end one day. I saw Brendan coming down the other side of Baggot Street, and had stiffened in anticipation of our ongoing cold war, but he began to sing the *Marseillaise*, and saluted me.

'Hello, John, let's join the French Foreign Legion, and free the world! And hump the begrudgers. *Formez vos bataillons, marchons, marchons!*'

*

We couldn't throw lavish parties in the basement of 6, Herbert Street. Despite its elegant proportions, it was a re-converted cellar and kitchen, much smaller than that infamous, bohemian warren called the Catacombs, described in *The Ginger Man*. And then there were the many little underground theatres of the period, like Captain Simpson's Pike and Liam Miller's Lantern: it was said then that you couldn't shove a load of coal into a basement without disrupting an avant-garde play. It now seems fascinating that Ireland's new intellectual and cultural life was fermenting in the cellars of elegant Anglo-Irish townhouses, the former landlord class being undermined literally from below.

Yet Madeleine and I could have intimate dinner parties; while the big table was always littered with papers, they could be shoved aside as, from her tiny kitchen, Madeleine conjured up flavoursome dishes, washed down by strong red wine from the French Embassy where she sometimes worked. When poet Tom Kinsella came, there was a bubbling *pot au feu* waiting for him, and the visionary American painter Morris Graves and his boyfriend enjoyed *coq au vin*. My salary was small enough, but Madeleine was inventive in a very French fashion. She was famous in Mulloy's of Baggot Street for always looking first in the buckets for anything they might have thrown out, splendid offal like brains or sweetbreads, or heart which she would stew with carrots, or black pudding with apples, which astounded Nelson Algren's Chicago palate. Home-made pâtés cooled on the window ledge.

Into this small, warm refuge came many literary pilgrims (as well as Madeleine's French relatives, a sister whose speciality was boneless chicken, her mother who could manage a dazzling *blanquette de veau*). After Algren, Sigal and Lessing, Ned O'Gorman came by, a Catholic Irish-American poet with an upper-class French mother, and of course Tom Parkinson again, to-ing and fro-ing from Berkeley, one of the first scholars to work on the Yeats poetry manuscripts, and something of a poet himself. He clashed with Ned, who disapproved when Tom read aloud from *Howl* by his protégé, Allen Ginsberg. Ned, with the communion wafer still crisp on his tongue, did not especially care to hear about being 'fucked in the ass by saintly motorcyclists'.

Parkinson stalked out into the night, growling about Americans with no social sense, and ran into Brendan, who took him to a dilapidated neighbourhood pub called the Beehive, reputed to have the most stinking outdoor privy in town, with a broken door and a flyblown interior which was rarely, if ever, hosed down. It was supposed to be closing time, but Brendan knew better, and they saw in the dawn, with a grateful Parkinson teaching Brendan the whole of *Howl*, which was much to Brendan's bisexual taste.

It had taken a while, however, for Brendan and Parkinson to get

CHAPTER ONE

along. It was the late 1950s, a period when Eisenhower's foreign and nuclear policies were not popular, and cries of 'American, go home!' could occasionally be heard even in the Dublin streets. It was a favourite taunt of Brendan's, but it died on his lips when he saw Parkinson approach, for Tom was an academic giraffe, a six-foot-seven, tennis-playing champion, and when he bounded through the wet streets of Dublin beneath a flaring umbrella it was quite a lofty sight. On his front steps at 15, Herbert Street, Brendan saw him coming, and began to launch a ritual attack, only to swallow his words and gasp admiringly, 'Jesus, Tom, it must be cold up there.'

I never saw Parkinson strike anyone, although he had a harsh temper, which, combined with his height, was enough to cow most people. But for me he had become an older brother and guide through the new writing which was emerging on the American West Coast. Indeed I had discovered an early poem of his in an edition of Cyril Connolly's *Horizon* when I was still a student, a poem called 'September Elegy', full of the lush warmth of California:

> Improbable California, the vineyard,
> all those apples,
> A world most fortunate and beautiful; and damned ...

*

The most stricken of all the does we sheltered in our small sanctuary was Ricki Huston, wife of film director John Huston. She was not only lovely, she was also very intelligent, at ease with our motley crew of writers, artists and scholars. She felt so welcome in that warm little space that she told me and Madeleine and a woman friend of ours why she felt so betrayed. A gifted ballet dancer (though a mere adolescent) she had abandoned her career to marry the much older John Huston, who had swept her off her feet with his customary casual élan. But it was just after she bore him a child, their daughter Anjelica, that she realised he would never be faithful; it was not in his character to provide the kind of fidelity that her own more vulnerable nature needed.

We also sheltered an Irish peer and his model-mistress. Some of these friends came through Madeleine's longing for her own class, but I was more than a little dubious about these new alliances, and when my Ulster Republican father heard of them he was furious, since he believed that the landlord class, the Planters, should all be burnt out like vermin. (I managed to turn the tables on my pious parents when I let them know that Madeleine was giving French lessons to the diminutive Papal Nuncio in his home in the Phoenix Park, and that he had invited us to share his box at the Dublin Horse Show.) But marriage is a series of adjustments, a process of growth through emotional exchange, and if Madeleine could swallow the tactlessness of some of my friends and relatives, my parents' acid comments on her childlessness, I could swallow some of her 'peers'. And in the newly emerging Ireland, all classes and kinds got thrown together, as I discovered at our first Christmas house party in Luggala, the home of Oonagh Guinness, Lady Oranmore and Browne.

It was a memorable evening, with Brendan bawling *The Old Triangle* at one end of the table, a Latin American playboy at the other, and the travelling singer, Margaret Barry, twanging her banjo in the middle: '*Her lovely hair hung down her face/And she was dressed in green ...*' Imagine a long dining table of distinguished guests, many of whom, like Cyril Connolly, and Caroline and Lucien Freud, represented the cream of artistic London, having

CHAPTER ONE

their senses assaulted by such wild Irish warblings as, '*She sang her song as she strolled along / And her name was Granuaille.*'

Margaret Barry had been invited, along with her fiddler fancy man, by tow-haired Garech Browne, a son of the house. Garech was to become one of my lifelong friends and collaborators, although it took me a while to overcome my inherited aversion to his archaic upper-class demeanour and to realise that there was a real mind under the seeming foppery. Some time after that riotous Christmas party, the telephone shrilled in our little apartment, and I heard Garech's cavalier tones.

'I know it's an unusual request,' he said, 'but could I borrow your wife for the evening?'

What happened afterwards led to a libel action, the foundation of a new company called Claddagh Records, and a friendship with the composer, Sean Ó Riada, but that is another story, or chronicle, or romp, to be continued later.

Meanwhile, I was completing my own first slim volume, *Forms of Exile*, which I hoped to get published before I reached the terrible age of thirty. Liam Miller of the Dolmen Press lived and worked only a stone's throw away, with his home in 94, Lower Baggot Street and his office in Mount Street near the Peppercannister Church. Gaunt and bearded as a Talmudic scholar, Liam was a book designer and printer of genius, whose lovely work, produced from his basement offices, was beginning to revive and transform the face of Irish poetry, which badly needed it.

CHAPTER TWO

SCYLLA AND CHARYBDIS

For make no mistake about it, when I was starting out, in the early 1950s, *all* the senior Irish poets (except MacNeice, because of Faber) were neglected. Clarke might intone on 'Radio Iran' (Kavanagh's acidly deliberate malapropism on *Radio Eireann*), or Kavanagh himself groan like an angry foghorn through Grafton Street, but they were not in print. And not only were their books more or less unavailable, but they were also fighting among themselves, like Kilkenny cats. Yet perhaps partly because of that strife, at the end of the decade Irish poetry was again in full sail, for the first time since the death of Yeats in 1939.

In 1950, *Anno Santo*, the Holy Year, I was twenty-one, with my heart set on going to Rome by way of Paris, Salzburg, Vienna and Venice. 'Matter-a-dam' that I had very little money: I was on my way. Brendan Behan had given me a few addresses in Paris, but beyond that I was on my own, which was the way I wanted it. For Ireland, and its capital, Dublin, seemed to me 'a fen of stagnant waters' (or writers) for someone like myself who wished to write poetry and/or prose. So I shook the rust of Ireland off my feet, and hied away for a few crucial months to explore broken post-war Europe, and discover my own proper loneliness. There is a melancholy sequence by my friend Michael Hamburger, called 'Notes of a European Tramp', which shows that my gloom was part of a generation:

> As for my heart, it broke some time ago
> when, in the towns of Europe, I still tried
> to live like other men and not to know
> that all we lived for had already died ...

Meanwhile, back in Dublin, the poetry wars were hotting up. Decades are untidy things, and the first salvo had really been fired by Kavanagh, in an extraordinary essay on Yeats's pal, F. R. Higgins, which bewildered me when I read it, during a lecture in the old UCD Physics Theatre. Called 'The Gallivanting Poet', it was published in our solitary literary magazine, *Irish Writing 3*, produced in Cork by a thoughtful young man, David Marcus, whose family belonged to Cork's once-flourishing Jewish community. 'The Gallivanting Poet' seemed to argue that Higgins was fake, because he was a Protestant pretending to be a Celtic Catholic, a new kind of sectarianism which threw me off balance because, although I was from Ulster, I had never imagined to encounter such ferocious bias in literary criticism. A mid-century chiliasm throbbed behind the words: 'Now is the time for silent prayer and long fasting. Literature as we have known it has come to the end of its tether.' It was followed by a similar attack in our leading monthly, *The Bell*, on Frank O'Connor, 'Coloured Balloons', challenging his authenticity as a recorder of Irish life.

Shortly after I returned from my mini *wanderjahre* in late 1950, a new magazine, *Envoy*, began, with Kavanagh (whom Val Iremonger, its poetry editor, called Kafka) blasting and bombadiering in its 'Diary'. Walking along Grafton Street in the company of another young poet, I saw a large shambling man, hat shoved on his head, plunging down the other side of the street. 'That's Patrick Kavanagh,' announced my companion, 'I *hate* that man!' Clearly, no one could be indifferent to this uncompromising figure, but unlike my fellow poet I felt obscurely drawn to him, as I tried to fathom the Irish poetry scene.

Kavanagh was striving towards a definition of the authentic in Irish life, through an analysis of its opposite, something called 'buck lepping', a strident form of Irishness that played to the gallery. *Envoy* collapsed, and was followed by the more satirical *Kavanagh's Weekly*, a blistering broadside subsidised by Kafka's brother, Peter. I recall a strange meeting with Patrick and the brother in Bewley's café that summer, both showing their big toes in outsize sandals.

'You're a very nervous young man,' flapped Kavanagh, 'but I wouldn't be surprised if you had *some* merit.'

We discussed a possible contribution by me, but he was already wearying of using the blunderbuss and bludgeon: 'Satire is a double-edged sword, it cuts the hand that wields it.' Peter Kafka was silent, dismissive of me, an almost unpublished young idealist.

Kavanagh was not writing poetry at the time: he was clearing the decks, seemingly in order to walk the plank, to use Hubert Butler's ironic metaphor for the cul de sac in which Kavanagh found himself after ranting against all the other Irish poets. But when his admirer and friend, Anthony Cronin, became assistant editor of the revived *Bell*, he and Peadar O'Donnell began to coax poems out of Kavanagh with hard cash, rueful revelations like 'Prelude' which express the self-criticism I had sensed:

> Give us another poem, they said
> Or they will think your muse is dead,

CHAPTER TWO

> Another middle-aged departure
> Of Apollo from the trade of archer.

Kavanagh's campaign routed the champions of the Irish or neo-Gaelic mode. Robert Farren, whose work Kavanagh described in his *Envoy* Diary as 'frivolity laid on with a navvy shovel', fell silent, although his *First Exile* (1944), a long poem on Colmcille, had been a big success, and his *Course* (now called *Curse* in the pub) *of Irish Verse* was a textbook for advocates of the Irish mode. Austin Clarke was also under fire. His conservative Cultural Relations pamphlet, *Poetry in Modern Ireland* (1951), which scanted Kavanagh and elevated F.R. Higgins and Farren, aroused great ire among the troops in McDaid's, Dublin's new bohemian pub.

For the poetic wars had spread to the pubs, where Irish writers were moving after the slow demise of the dignified *salons* of the Literary Revival. During the isolation of the War years, euphemistically called 'the Emergency', most writers congregated in the lofty-ceilinged Palace Bar: there is a famous photograph of the 'standing army' of Irish writers. As the ideological divide grew, the older writers moved to the Pearl, across from the *Irish Times*, while the young consorted with Kavanagh in the more *farouche* McDaid's. Or so it seemed, but human affairs are always more complicated: John Jordan exchanged affectionate obscenities with Kavanagh, Cronin discussed racing form, Myles (alias Flann O'Brien) scowled, Pearse Hutchinson praised yet another book, Brendan Behan trotted through, and I even dared to enter myself. It was a scene that would be well described by Valentin Iremonger in the anonymous *Leader* profile of Kavanagh, which led to Kavanagh's unwise libel action.

What was the root of these wars? It was an Irish version of the perennial dispute between the Ancient and the Modern, involving one step forward and one step back. In the *Faber Book of Contemporary Irish Verse* (1949), Valentin Iremonger and Robert Greacen declared themselves for a multiplicity of styles. Iremonger, a lean Dublin diplomat with a slight cast in one eye, had been the apostle of the Modern in Ireland, with articles in *The Bell* on the major contemporary British poets. But when someone like MacNeice did come through, with his side-kick W.R. Rodgers, it was usually to record BBC radio programmes on the past, on the great dead figures of the Literary Revival. They were a dangerously seductive pair to meet, the lean intelligent face of MacNeice, Rodgers' deceptively gentle sibilance, as they cruised all day through Dublin, from the Tower bar (the Radio Eireann pub in Henry Street) to the Pearl; I once saw MacNeice slumped in McDaid's, although that was much later. But the real centre of the maelstrom was the outsize personality of Patrick Kavanagh.

Was Kavanagh really so large? (I am six foot myself, and while I used be intent and skinny, I have grown ample with age: according to a recent interview in the *Irish Times*, burly as a 'veritable lumberjack'.) Or was it more the way he spread himself, awkwardly and untidily? In *Dead as Doornails*, Anthony Cronin quotes a marvellous comment of Kavanagh's father, to the effect that his son must be a poet, because he broke everything on the farm except the crowbar, and he managed to bend that. Anyway, one was always aware of his physical presence: despite his huddled posture, he did not gather into his corner, but seemed to expand from it. And he did have large feet and hands, a large head and a strong voice, which one can hear on our first Claddagh speech record, *Almost Everything*. You always knew he was there, and when he sang during his special UCD lectures, or late at night after the pub, that lonely, one-lunged sound was heartbreaking:

> If ever you go to Dublin town
> In a hundred years or so
> Inquire for me in Baggot Street
> And what I was like to know ...

In 1953 I took off again, this time to America, where I had been born in the first year of the Depression. Ireland seemed to be the Slough of Despond, with Kavanagh growing more grumpy, and *The Bell* tolling more dimly for a second time: Cronin's editorials of the period sound like a foghorn in thick mist, as if the island were drowning. This coming and going was part of the decade, as we sought to come to terms with our sour little country. Hutchinson and Jordan had found a refuge in Barcelona, and Cronin was soon to leave too, for a longer time in southern Spain.

When I came back three years later, things had begun to get better, mainly because of Liam Miller and his Dolmen Press, the first poetry press in Ireland since the Cuala, and with an equally high standard of design. They had produced Tom Kinsella's first frail book, *Poems* (1956) and would foster his *Another September* (1958), the first Irish book to be a Choice of the Poetry Book Society. And Clarke was being reluctantly reborn, perhaps in response to all the taunts, the hostile atmosphere. *Ancient Lights* (1955) gathered together older favourites like 'The Blackbird of Derrycairn', from his play *The Crow Flies*, but also introspective, angry poems like 'Ancient Lights', to be followed in two years by *Too Great a Vine*, which contains my favourite Clarke longer poem,

'The Loss of Strength', compressing our early religious history with glittering technique:

> Too great a vine, they say, can sour
> The best of clay. No pair of sinners
> But learned saints had overpowered
> Our country, Malachi the Thin
> And Bernard of Clairvaux. Prodigious
> In zeal, these cooled and burned our porridge.
> (Later came breakspear, strong bow backing)
> The arch sprang wide for their Cistercians.
> O bread was wersh and well was brack.
> War rattled at us in hammered shirts:
> An Englishman had been the Pontiff.
> They marched to Mellifont.

Although most of my day was taken up with my editorial job at Bord Failte, the Irish Tourist Board (the only job I could find), I was beginning to assemble my own slim first volume, *Forms of Exile* (1958). Between the Scylla of craftsman Clarke and the Charybdis of an angry Kavanagh, I had lived out my Irish poetic 1950s, and now things were looking up. I recall a series of readings in the Eblana Theatre, probably the first public performances by poets for a long time; it seems that Kavanagh never gave a poetry reading in his life, dying just before what Cronin exasperatedly calls 'the great Poetry Boom'. People assumed the usual masks of deference to conceal their boredom and unease, but when Kinsella read 'Baggot Street Deserta', even the Chairman, President of Galway University Paddy Browne, woke up: 'It's great to hear such intelligent poetry again.' 'The window is wide / On a crawling arch of stars.'

CHAPTER TWO

I read with Maire Mhac an tSaoi, part (with Sean O Riordain and Mairtin O Direain) of the New Wave of Irish poetry in Irish, which had come alive again during the War years when Ireland drew back into herself. And with Patrick Galvin, whose 'My Little Red Knife' sent shudders through the more respectable sections of the audience: Miss O'Flaherty of Parsons book shop shook her metaphorical rosary at him when he read lines like 'I kissed and kissed a thousand lies/And opened wide her golden thighs/To please my little red knife'. Galvin had been working in England, but he and Ewart Milne were to return to swell the new poetry scene. There were still few women, and they tended to be 'lady poets'. I knew that delicate pianist, Rhoda Coghill, whose 'Bright Hillside' I admired. And there were Freda Laughton and Temple Lane, mild pioneers of a story still to be told. Brendan Behan's future grandmother-in-law, Blanaid Salkeld, published *Experiment in Error* (1958), at the age of seventy-five. And speaking of Brendan, few might realise that he launched his own literary career as *Brendan O Beachain*, a writer of plangent poems in Irish. Nearly ten years after Iremonger's Faber anthology, a new *Oxford Book of Irish Verse*, edited by Donagh MacDonagh and Lennox Robinson, tried to close the floodgates by limiting the inclusion of the younger poets (including myself), but the 1960s had already begun.

CHAPTER THREE

AS GOOD AS A PLAY, OR, A HUMAN BEHAN

> The pubs shut: a released bull,
> Behan shoulders up the street,
> topples into our basement, roaring 'John!'
> from 'Herbert Street Revisited'

I liked Brendan Behan. It seems important to say this, because much that has been written and spoken about him, especially by his Irish contemporaries, is surprisingly hostile. Once, listening to a Radio Eireann programme of sour reminiscences, I could not recognise my ebullient, generous and witty friend: the compassion which he extended so often to others was not being granted to him. Anthony Cronin's account in *Dead as Doornails* begins the dismantling of the legend, and to give Cronin his due, he may have been trying to analyse the dangers inherent in Brendan's stage Irish persona, that myth of the irreverent, hard-drinking writer which engulfed Brendan's real self, as it had Dylan Thomas's. As for the American sailor who claims to have been Brendan's lover, his account is loveless. There have been two professional biographies, which I will come to later. But first I would like to extend a warm hand to my old friend and neighbour, the 'sole proprietor of the biggest heart that has beaten in Ireland in the last forty years', according to Flann O'Brien, a writer not usually given to the lavish compliment.

Brendan Behan and I first crossed paths amicably enough, in the dank, threadbare Dublin of the late 1940s and early 1950s, usually in pubs. I was learning how to drink, the only acceptable form of revolt in those censor-and-cleric-ridden days, but I did not haunt the Catacombs, that late-night warren of drink and debauchery, described by both Donleavy and Cronin; dance halls and young women were higher on my youthful list of priorities. Indeed Donleavy's account of Brendan's entrance in *The Ginger Man* may be the first literary glimpse of his rambunctious presence, as he strides into that infamous basement, declaring, 'And you lovely women. The fine builds of ye. I'd love to do you all and your young brothers.' Or else affectionately threatening to beat one young man to death with bound copies of the *Catholic Herald*.

And I was not really part of the *Envoy* magazine crowd, which gathered in McDaid's, although the poetry editor, Valentin Iremonger, did squeeze a poem of mine past Kavanagh and his cohorts. But Brendan and Val were real pals, the house painter and the diplomat usually falling into Irish, to foil any hostile listeners. Brendan had studied Irish in prison in the Curragh, where he had attended a class given by the great Irish writer, Martín Ó Cadháin. So the Brendan I first read was the poet in Irish, author of lyrics as delicate as Japanese, which distil a solitude sharpened by years in prison. 'A blunt and numbing pain it is, to wake up in a cell…' he sighs in *Borstal Boy*, and speaks of '*Uagineas gan ciuneas*, loneliness without peace':

> In the silent cell
> The train's chill whistle

> A couple's laughter
> To the lonely one.
>
> The tang of blackberries
> Wet with rain
> On the hilltop.
> *(Translation: John Montague)*

And of course we shared a passion for France. When I was setting out, in 1950, on a rather unorthodox version of a Holy Year Pilgrimage, Brendan gave me several addresses in Paris. I used only the first, a Monsieur Pierre, patron of a café in the rue Jacob, but it was a humdinger. I found myself drinking champagne with Pierre and a shell-shocked Belgian, who despised the French so much for their capitulation to the Germans that he was determined to get rid of all his francs, as if they were scorching his pockets. Presently, Monsieur Pierre conducted us to a 'good house', where we got more than bed and board for a long weekend. The Belgian veteran presided over the Sunday dinner, with whores to the right and left of him, and the Madame at the other end. As the rough red flowed, we grew merrier and merrier, like characters in a Maupassant story, dancing and singing, punctuated by cries of '*Les lâches*!' when the Belgian blearily recalled his wartime experience of the fleeing French army.

It was my maiden voyage, and probably the Belgian's last. Heady stuff for a twenty-one year old Ulster Catholic, and Brendan enjoyed the story when I finally got back, complimenting me on discovering one of the last unofficial whorehouses in Montmartre, where the old friendly atmosphere still prevailed despite their official closing in 1948. But he rebuked me for using only the more

CHAPTER THREE

frivolous address; I should also have called on Mark Mortimer at the British Institute.

'There's more to Paris than *bordels*,' Brendan said sternly, 'Mark really knows Paris. You might have learnt something worthwhile.'

What really interested Brendan were my impressions of life on the Left Bank, which was then the intellectual capital of post-war Europe. The underground clubs like the Tabou, and the Rose Rouge, where Juliette Greco sang, the terraces of the 'Maggots' or the Mabillon, were all well known to Brendan. And they had already heard of him as a writer: Sinbad Vail, son of Peggy Guggenheim, had printed Brendan's delicate story 'After the Wake' in his magazine *Points*, though Brendan later repudiated it because it exposed his liking for boys. In the exuberant bohemian atmosphere of Saint Germain, where Genet and Baldwin were leading lights, and Gide was the local Nobel laureate, no one cared a 'fig' about homosexuality. But back in melancholy Dublin, such sexual diversity was dangerous, and the naturally loquacious Brendan had to try to keep his mouth shut.

Brendan's sexuality was complex and seldom fulfilled. He liked women, but his early years in prison had given him a feeling for the fine manly forms of his fellow felons. He confided to me that what he would really like was 'a boy on top of a girl, and myself on top of that,' a pyramid not easily choreographed in the pious Ireland of our youth, or indeed, anywhere west of Bangkok.

(He vouchsafed this confidence when a group of us younger writers and actors had moved to the bar of Westland Row railway station, which, like all the mainline station bars, remained open throughout the afternoon. Ironically, in such a hard-drinking city, the pubs maintained rigid licensing hours, so dedicated imbibers had to be resourceful. The ordinary pubs closed every afternoon from half-past two to half-past three for the 'Holy Hour', to let the 'curates' or barmen have their lunch. The further irony of this religious terminology should not escape us, 'curates' serving spirits to those who pushed up to the counter in an unconscious parody of the Mass. And Brendan's murmured confidences to me over our chalices were like a Confession.)

It is contrary to Brendan's legend, but timidity, probably related to his sexual ambiguity, was also part of his problem. His stammer betrayed his double nature, not only his sexual conflict, but the basic gentleness beneath the public bluster. According to our mutual friend and contemporary, the Dublin writer and critic John Jordan, in the magazine *Hibernia*, the 'roistering, brazen-tongued public entertainer was merely the defensive obverse of the warm-hearted, generous, slightly unsure friend'. There was also the class, or social issue: he was uneasy with the fluent University wits who formed the new wave of Irish writing in the 1950s. Brendan might be accepted in Paris, but the McDaid's lot were not always so generous, regarding him as a coarse-mouthed intruder. Patrick Kavanagh was both afraid and increasingly jealous of Behan's growing reputation, and Kavanagh was king, so Brendan's prose work-in-progress languished in various editorial offices. There was, as well, the tension between city and country, Brendan's urban or 'jackeen' disdain for what he called 'bogmen' or 'culchies', anyone born beyond Dublin city limits. Which would include Kavanagh, affectionately known to all as 'the Monaghan wanker' because of a notorious passage in his wonderful long poem, *The Great Hunger*. Brendan's scorn was partly a comic ploy, because he loved the Kerry and Connemara *gaeltachts*; in fact, one of his most beautiful early poems is a lament for the death of the Blasket Island Irish-speaking communities: 'A Jackeen Keens for the Blaskets'. I think it is one of the most plangent

CHAPTER THREE

poems of my generation, in either language, and certainly belies the myth of Behan as an insensitive lout.

Brendan was sore about all this, because, as we can now clearly see, *Borstal Boy* was the only major prose work produced at the time, along with Donleavy's *The Ginger Man*. Even Kavanagh's great late poems would come only after he gave up haranguing his public and began to laze along the Grand Canal, relinquishing his 'culchie' persona for a Dublin one, Baggot Street and its environs becoming his new parish in poem and song. As I myself was trying to grope my way through the intellectual murk of literary Dublin without being gored, I was sympathetic to Brendan's frustration. He was the only young writer amongst us who had a real subject matter, and his reading in three languages was impressive. Indeed, he was the only trilingual bisexual I have ever met. He had translated Brian Merriman and could recite yards of Yeats and Auden, as well as Paul Eluard, the lyric conscience of French communism. His Dublin socialist background gave him a more international context and culture than most of us, but supposedly he was not sensitive enough to appreciate poetry. Yet his mother, Kathleen, had known Maud Gonne, and used to sing the poems of A. E. Housman, and Stephen, the 'da', was a dab hand at the story-telling, reading his children everything from Dickens to the *Decameron*. Still, some of the easily-threatened McDaid's lot could not understand this rich inheritance, could not reconcile Brendan's unabashedly working-class accent, dress and demeanour with their notions of how an intellectual should behave. They could stomach Kavanagh's bad manners because he was an older writer of achieved genius, but Brendan was still in brilliant embryo.

Brendan fought back against his sharp-tongued detractors, but I knew he was stung by their malice, a problem we both shared. In the Dublin of the time, you had to be the fastest word alive in order to survive, but, like me, Brendan hadn't the heart for real acrimony, for the words that kill. 'When I am in good humour, I could not be bitter about anything,' he maintains in *Borstal Boy*. And, as well as an admiration for things French, we had the secret complicity of stammerers, whose halting speech betrays their vulnerability. We only really talked when alone together, all too aware of the distorting acoustics around us. We met more often when I moved to an old rambling Georgian flat near the Gloucester Diamond and the Five Lamps, on Dublin's North Side, territory of 'Spike' McCormack and the Animal Gang. It was also on the edge of Joyce's Night Town, and although the new Irish State had abolished the 'kips' or 'brochels', there were still many stray ladies in the shadows between Saville Place and O'Connell Street. I came to know some of my unorthodox neighbours, and, when one could find no more lucrative billet, I would sometimes give a lady-in-waiting a bed for the night, and cook her breakfast in the morning.

Brendan was impressed by the strange goings-on in my gaunt Georgian flat, two big airy rooms and a sprawling kitchen below, with the sound of shunting trains from Amiens Street station echoing through my increasingly uneasy sleep. 'You're a quare one,' he said admiringly. 'Film critic for the *Catholic Standard* and running a whores' hostel.'

My stint at the *Standard* stretched over two years, before I was sacked for a too-outspoken contribution to *The Bell*. Then, after a brief attempt to return to Irish academic life, I achieved my ambition of withdrawing from the now claustrophobic gloom of Dublin, through a Fulbright Fellowship that would take me to America. I bought Brendan a few parting glasses during the Holy Hour in Amiens Street station. (We were riding herd on a young actor called

CHAPTER THREE

Jack MacGowran, who was on a serious tear, or binge, and might need our help later: Brendan was great like that, offering succour to those in a worse state than himself.) He was more morose than complimentary about my good news.

'I suppose you'd expect congratulations or that class of thing, but you're going to be fed and housed in your Ivy League University. The only institutions that ever looked after me were prisons. And now I'll be left alone with the rest of these middle-class University fuckers. Only a year or so up from the bogs and the stirabout, and they're already knee-deep in the angst, Kafka-ing and Rilke-ing like mad. Jaysus, they put years on you. Don't forget to come back,' he admonished, raising his familiar war-cry with his glass, 'And hump the begrudgers!'

In the meantime, Jack had curled into a ball in the corner to sleep, from which we would rouse him a few hours later, since he would have to appear on the Abbey stage that evening. He would have sobered up, but we would be tipsy from nursemaiding him.

*

When we re-met three years later, in 1954, we were both young married men, and, by lucky chance, living more or less side by side, in Dublin's genteel Herbert Street. It was noticeable that Brendan was migrating steadily from the North Side slums of his youth to the more sedate south, perhaps in a curve towards respectability?

Few people think of Behan as a husband, but that was the role in which I finally came to know him best. And my own wife took to him immediately, as she was meant to. When they first met, as Madeleine and I were walking by the misty Canal, he surprised her by asking if he could put his finger in her mouth.

'Bite, daughter,' he cried, 'bite as hard as you can, on the knuckle.'

A surprised Madeleine did as she was instructed, until Brendan's face whitened.

'Jaysus, girl, you're a fine specimen, and may you have fine children. But,' he continued, his eyes narrowing with mischief, 'do you know what you've gone and done? You've married an Ulsterman. A grand girl like yourself, you'd expect a bit of appreciation and affection. But all you'll get from one of that lot is a pair of cold feet in the bed.'

Then he launched into a fluent stream of street French, which delighted her exile's heart; she found his command of *argot* unusual and impressive.

Brendan was now at the height of his powers, a formidable little bull crackling with energy and affection for the world. A trip to the Markets for an early morning cure, home to a heavy breakfast, a few hours hammering at his antediluvian typewriter: that was how he completed *Borstal Boy* and began *The Hostage*, plus a new novel that opened sensationally: 'There was a party to celebrate Deirdre's return from her abortion in Bristol.' If he spent the rest of the day in the pubs, it seemed a natural enough reward, and, if you caught him early enough, there would be a gas session.

One hilarious afternoon sticks in my mind. When my sweet though quite sober wife left for Paris to see her family, I was liable to go on the tear, since my office job at Bord Failte was a necessary evil which bored and constrained me. And since Brendan was more or less permanently on the tear himself in the afternoons, we would team up in search of devilment. In a pub in Baggot Street, across from Parsons book shop, we met the then Lord Mayor of Dublin, who was taking a breather between two public ceremonies. Brendan

CHAPTER THREE

and I plunged into the poetry, reciting Auden and Yeats at the tops of our voices, while plying the Lord Mayor with drink until his head began to droop towards the counter. At this point Brendan decided that since the man was jarred in the course of his official duties, we should purloin his Chain of Office for safety's sake, and also so that the insignia of Brendan's native city should not be disgraced by a mayoral booze hound. So off with us through the town, with protesting officials in confused pursuit. Brendan was wearing the Chain across his open-necked shirt, bawling out ballads, and declaring that he was Dublin's first citizen. And that I was its last, because I had two strikes against me, being a bogman and also from the frozen North. For every song he sang, I had to recite a poem, and I remember him standing to attention as I recited Auden's 'In Memory of W. B. Yeats' in a pseudo-Oxford accent. 'You were *silly*... Your gift survived it *all*... '

'He writes well for a middle-class limey, the condescending fucker,' said Brendan admiringly.

We did not discuss writing much, but there was mutual respect despite the disparity in our achievements; Brendan's fame was now world-wide, and I was only getting back to real writing after three years of wandering and teaching in the States. If I published a poem or review, he usually managed to find something decent to say about it, although he still smarted from what he regarded as the unfair treatment he had received. Dubliners like Iremonger, Jimmy Plunkett and even John Jordan he always spoke well of, but beyond the *lingua franca* of Dublin men oppressed and besieged by culchies, there was his simple belief that writing was something sacred. He might joke about it, as he did about everything else, but it was what mattered. 'You may roll in the gutter, as long as you don't destroy the gift.' It seemed to me then a very romantic attitude, but later I came to regard it as almost a prophetic summary of his descent into the toils of self-destruction.

Another time that Madeleine innocently left for Paris to visit her august military family, I took 'French leave' from the office, crossing Brendan's path in various hostelries, including McDaid's. Indeed, I brought half of McDaid's home one night, distributing the bodies as they fell, some even on the marital bed, with myself sprawled on the sofa. Brendan came trotting by in the morning, perhaps on his way home from the Markets after an early morning tincture, and glimpsed the strewn bodies, the distinctly un-French disorder, through our window. The door had been left open, so he sidled in to inspect the damage, and I blearily felt him hovering above my face.

'Jaysus, John, you've lost your looks,' he said. 'You should give up the drink. And what about the job?'

Shortly after, he brought us all up to Number 15, his own flat, for a restorative breakfast of bacon, eggs and pots of strong tea, with Beatrice cooking and him serving, a white towel over his arm.

Madeleine was only dimly aware of these goings-on whenever the harness was briefly taken off. But she had a succession of mad uncles who were prone to get a bit blasted themselves and complain about their lives, since they were a dying breed, the last of a French warrior class. So she was used to succouring the sodden male, and had a special family recipe, a kind of strong gruel, to settle a drink-scourged stomach. Only she had never thought that she would have to use it in Ireland, and with her own husband. I defeated her best intentions when, at the Bord Failte Christmas party, I determined to keep up with the boys. The advertising staff in particular were hardened whiskey drinkers, and after about round twelve I began to falter, just managing to ring Madeleine before I fell. She dutifully came to Phil Ryan's pub to prop me home; but as she steered me into Herbert Street she had to pass Beatrice Behan, sweeping the litter off her doorstep. Beatrice gave the embarrassed Madeleine a commiserating look, a memory which still makes Madeleine wince ruefully.

Despite his routine excesses, I was nearly always exhilarated by Brendan's marvellous Wildean wit that could conjure adventure from the air. But there were already disquieting aspects. *The Quare Fellow* had made him famous, from its first production in the tiny Pike Theatre in the lane behind Herbert Street. It was our local theatre, and we could drop in whenever we felt like it; I helped Captain Simpson remove Brendan from the premises when he fell into a drunken sleep during a rehearsal. And I remember the Number 10 bus shuddering to a halt in the middle of Baggot Street Bridge while a very drunk Brendan lurched down, helped by an exasperated but relieved conductor. Supporting him down the street, I wondered what was wrong?

Ever since I had met him, Brendan had been working on a memoir of prison life, and the failure of his contemporaries to appreciate it was his most long-standing hurt. I gathered that parts of it had been submitted to *Envoy* and *The Bell*; Anthony Cronin, associate editor of *The Bell* at that time, acknowledges their rejection of Behan in his own memoir, in which, astonishingly, he describes Brendan's book as 'doubtless a work of near genius'. I would agree with Cronin's praise, because the passages Brendan showed me glowed with energy, a quality sadly lacking in those slack years. He always had pages in his coat pocket, and the unpublished manuscript grew and grew, until Ian Hamilton of Hutchinson came to Dublin scouting for material, and the ever-faithful Iremonger immediately put him on to Behan. One day Brendan proudly confronted me with a mountain of typescript.

'It's off to my London publisher tomorrow,' he proclaimed. 'I might let you help me with the proofs, since after all those schools you must know how to read.'

I was eager to help, but when he bounced them into my lap many months later, he was driven more by a yearning for applause than by any real need for editorial advice. I read it carefully over a weekend, but when I produced my suggestions, he was impatient. The wait and the hurt had lasted too long; he now craved instant recognition.

Despite a faltering of interest towards the end, and a tendency to repetition, *Borstal Boy* is a formidable achievement, in the tradition of the Irish jail journal, a lewd commentary on John Mitchell. And, with *The Quare Fellow*, it made Brendan the most prominent writer of his generation in Ireland. *The Hostage* is more controversial, and many Irish-speaking critics regard it as a betrayal of *An Giall*, his original version in Irish. However, Brendan made it clear to me that he was not happy with *An Giall*, and spoke of taking it away to 'make a real play out of it'. He seemed to regard the Irish-speaking audience in the Damer Theatre as limited in their appreciation, to feel that they could only digest something simplistic, with suitably patriotic sentiments. This is not a fair view of *An Giall*, which has a delicate pathos, but I have no doubt that Brendan disliked intensely the direction of Frank Dermody, whose idea of theatre he found too old-fashioned and naturalistic. There may also have been a clash of personalities; Dermody's manner was fussy and precise, qualities one would not usually associate with Brendan.

Besides, Dermody was connected with the Abbey Theatre, which had rejected his first play, *The Quare Fellow*, on two different

CHAPTER THREE

occasions. The Abbey was then in its 'Queen's Theatre' limbo, between the partial burning of the old morgue, and the new plush Abbey of the more stylish 1960s. It was fashionable among Irish intellectuals to deplore the Abbey's standards of production, and indeed most of the plays I saw there have sunk out of sight. But Brendan's objection was more deep-rooted; he lamented the lack of freedom, the conventionality, of the Irish theatre. Even the flamboyant Micheal MacLiammoir did not satisfy him. We met after MacLiammoir's one-man show of *The Importance of Being Earnest*, and Brendan was scathing about the coy reticence of the text. 'You'd think Oscar was in prison for stealing an apple.'

He loved the new London theatre, the excitement of the Royal Court, the mixture of musical comedy and social comment developed by Joan Littlewood at the Theatre Royal, which suited both his socialist beliefs and his own theatrical inheritance. He complained that Joan Littlewood had worked him very hard, but I have rarely seen him happier than on that First Night of *The Hostage*, October 1958; I was there with Doris Lessing and Clancy Sigal. Brendan was as sober as a judge, stylishly confined in a dress suit, and I have rarely heard a better curtain speech. The audience took the production the way it was intended, as a serious romp, a modern tragi-comedy, the first 'play kit', with a compelling central theme, and room for social embroidery depending on place and time.

*

During those early years of marriage, Brendan tried his best to harness his demons. He was very proud of Beatrice and her extraordinary capacity, at least at the beginning, for quiet amusement at his antics, even when they were sometimes excessive. There is a lovely picture of him crushing his great animal head against her pale face, and his imitation of her, brush in hand before her easel, was one of his new party tricks, in addition to The Old Woman of the Roads, The Trial of Oscar Wilde, and Toulouse Lautrec, for which he would wear his shoes backwards on bent knees. If the daughter had arrived earlier, I am convinced that Brendan would have lived, because he loved children as much as or more than he desired young men. I have a favourite image of him festooned with children at Blackrock Baths, performing elaborate belly flops for their delight. And whenever Madeleine's pretty little niece came to stay with us, Brendan would fire bags of *bon-bons* through the window, '*pour la petite*'.

By eerie coincidence, my first marriage was also childless, and I recall a sadly hilarious exchange with Brendan cross-examining the novelist Benedict Kiely, in genuine puzzlement, as to how he had managed to have so many children, while Ben mumbled some vague consolation. It was as if he truly believed that he might be doing something wrong in the love department. For, despite the casual exchanges that sometimes prevailed in Dublin's bohemia, we actually knew very little about sex in those days. And certainly almost nothing about problems like infertility, which even doctors discussed in hushed tones.

In my experience, in a childless marriage there is a tendency to revert to former habits, because the anchor that children provide is missing. It was the tension between Brendan and Beatrice in this area that began to tear at the heart of their marriage, as it had begun to trouble my own, albeit less seriously, perhaps because my French wife could speak more candidly about sexual matters than most Irish people at that time.

Brendan dropped in on us most nights for a last drink – 'a wee, wee sup', he would implore in stage-Irish tones, holding up the glass like a chalice – before heading home. One night, he had either drained the bottle earlier, or found it empty. He took this as an insult, angry words were exchanged, and I threw him out, or rather up our basement flight, not an easy task on a wet night, and with a sullen, drunken Brendan on my hands. But club football and my mother's pub had given me some basic bouncer skills, and I rammed his sodden, thirteen-stone bulk up the steps, his oaths fouling the air. As a last salute, he turned to kick me in the face, but I caught his heel and toppled him into the street. I feared we might consider our friendship at an end, but he never mentioned the matter again; if you put manners on him, he respected you. And although he had a street-fighter's repertoire of dirty tricks, he was by that time usually too befuddled to use it.

Indeed, in another episode, during a Christmas party at Luggala, I had to come to his aid. Accused of intruding into the children's bedroom (something easy to do by mistake in that house of curving corridors, especially if you were a bit tipsy and looking for a leak), he was being dealt with harshly by several more sober guests. He lay splayed on the cobbles of the courtyard in the snow, while a Latin American playboy – whose morals were far more dubious than Brendan's – kicked him mercilessly. I felt that Brendan might have taken him if he had been in any kind of shape, but, as well as being drunk, he did not seem to have the heart for it. I bundled him and Beatrice into a van and we barrelled home over the dawning Wicklow mountains. Once again, I found his bark worse than his bite. Despite his threats of 'putting the boys onto Miguel Ferreras', he seemed to have no appetite for real vengeance any more, worn down by years in prison and the self-punishment of alcoholism.

Flann O'Brien's obituary declares of Brendan that 'There has been no Irishman quite like him ... He exuded good nature ... (and was) the sole proprietor of the biggest heart that has beaten in Ireland in the last forty years.' Truly, his generosity was as outsize as his burly physique. You could hardly buy a drink, or even a meal, without him seizing the bill, or throwing a wad as thick as a cattle-dealer's on the table. And if he had drunk all your whiskey on his homeward halt the night before, he would usually call round with more, plus flowers and sweets, the next morning. I did not like the hangers-on that began to gather round him, taking all he could give but often reviling him behind his back. They would encourage him to perform, to make a scene of himself, and at such times I would often slip away. I only once asked him for real money.

As most young marrieds do, I had come up against a financial problem of a fairly conventional kind, but one which required a large, immediate loan, preferably without the strict conditions that a bank would impose. I braced myself to face Brendan, because I feared that money might soil our relationship, which had never been parasitical. So I stammered my request at the lunch hour one day, but I need not have worried; it was met with instant sympathy. He did not have a sum like that handy at the moment but he would have it in a day or two, and yes, the wives were to be kept out of it. In due course, he summoned me out of Bord Failte to the Beehive, and the money was pressed into my hand. He could not resist a moment of curiosity, perhaps in an effort to glamorise the tactful and undramatic exchange.

'For a cautious fukken Ulsterman you seem to have got yourself into a sizeable spot of trouble. No one could be up to you culchies. Tell me ...' He himself began to stammer, and to laugh mischievously. 'Did you get a g-g-goat into t-t-trouble?'

Nothing would do Brendan but to think that I was keeping a mistress, paying for an abortion, or buying rifles to liberate my native Tyrone (the 1950s campaign was still on). I managed to concoct an unlikely explanation, to gratify his appetite for myth: he could face quotidian fact but preferred a richly-coloured story. The anti-climax came when I returned the money a few months later; he had never mentioned it again, but I had made it clear that I considered it a loan. It was a cold winter evening, after work, when I handed him the payment. He fell into a gloomy silence, seeming almost hurt. I anxiously asked if I had been too slow, or upset him in any way.

'You have,' he growled. 'For now I'll go and fukken spend it. At least I felt I was doing some good with you, whatever it was. But trust a fukken Northerner. You can't recognise a present when you get one. At least I hope the girl is out of trouble.' Then he grinned. 'Maybe she'll have the sense to get shut of you.'

*

'He was as good as a play'
Flann O'Brien

One truly riotous exchange has never ceased to amuse me, as an example of Brendan at his wicked best. Tom Parkinson, the Yeats scholar and poet, was staying with us again, writing reports on Ireland for *The Nation*, which involved journeys North, since the 1950s IRA campaign was then at its peak. I can testify that Brendan, despite his Republican background, knew little about it. In fact, he was quite upset when Parkinson and I were roughly questioned by the RUC in Newry, which was very tense at that time, and under curfew: the bus station had been burned down the very night we arrived.

Readers will remember that Parkinson was around six-foot-seven, a grumpy scholarly sky scraper, extremely conspicuous in a vigilant border town amongst the medium-sized natives. In order to survey Parkinson, the RUC Inspector had to tilt his head dangerously back and clutch at his cap to prevent it falling off, which somewhat weakened his intimidating stance.

As well as the IRA campaign, Parkinson was interested in the Fethard-on-Sea controversy, during which Donal Barrington spoke out against the local boycott of Protestants, describing it as one of the most divisive incidents since the Civil War, 'an unjust and terrible thing'. As Donal, a future judge, had been a University classmate of mine, I asked him to dinner, so that our American friend could see that real liberals still existed in Ireland. We also had my wife's niece staying with us, the pretty little girl from Paris whom Brendan adored, but Brigitte was safely tucked up in bed, and conversation had begun to warm up to the main subject of Church and State in Ireland, when there came a knock at the door.

Madeleine and I exchanged apprehensive glances; it was too early for Brendan.

'Good God,' exclaimed my wife as she hurried to answer, 'it looks like a priest!'

And almost as though on cue, a shy but determined young man entered, announcing that he was our local curate, on his parish rounds.

'I've heard of you,' he said nervously, when Barrington was introduced, putting a damper on the occasion. The serious conversation had only just been kindling, but it nearly guttered out now, with Parkinson glowering at the clergyman, Barrington looking embarrassed, and Madeleine trying to be a gracious hostess, offering drink, which was duly refused since, he explained, he was local head

CHAPTER THREE

of the Pioneers (what Brendan mockingly called 'The Sacred Thirst'). Meanwhile, I searched desperately for harmless topics, and thought I had found one. Lately we had received many calls from the Legion of Mary, who seemed fascinated by our bohemian way of life, and were determined that God should be a part of it. I broached the matter lightly with Father Lee, but he took it seriously, like a man gripping a solitary oar on an uncertain sea.

'Oh, I must speak to the girls in that case: we can't have them upsetting people. Even if it is a good cause. They are very good people, you know.'

'Ah, don't worry, Father, I have worked out a way of dealing with them. I tell them that there's a man up the street who needs their help more than I do: Mr Behan at Number 15. And that they should try to induct him into the Pioneer Total Abstinence Association.'

'Oh, Mr Behan, the famous playwright,' the priest breathed. 'I've been looking forward to meeting him. He's one of my parishioners too: Westland Row is quite a big parish, you know.'

We all fell silent, contemplating his pious innocence in welcoming such a confrontation, when God decided that it should happen, for all our benefit. Suddenly, a second and more bulky body came clattering down the steps, and a fist banged at our door. Once more, Madeleine went to open, mumbling, 'Jesus, it *is* Brendan.' Behan barged past her, breathing heavily, with a kind of mock-heroic fire.

'I heard you,' he accused. ' "*Jesus, it* is *Brendan.*" You're becoming as foul-tongued as the rest of us fuckers.' He wagged his finger at her. 'Don't forget you have a child living with you, so you must give good example.'

Then he slowly took in the situation, the table with the remains of the abandoned dinner party, Parkinson like a kind of seated Eiffel Tower, to whom he nodded, and Barrington whom he had heard of, but could not immediately place. There was no Brigitte, so he dropped a bag of sweets on the table, and was turning to go, when he saw the priest, sitting tensely behind him, on the edge of his chair, smiling anxiously. Brendan looked at him with genuine and growing disbelief: he clearly had never associated our home with clerical interference. Finally he went cautiously over, as though to poke him with his toe to find out if he was real.

'In the name of God, Father, what holy water font did you spring out of?'

The young priest dealt manfully with Brendan's incredulity, taking the 'bull' by the horns, so to speak.

'You must be Mr Behan,' he said. 'I have been very much looking forward to calling on you. You are in my parish, you know, and of course I have heard of your work.'

Silence, while Brendan's brow swelled with disbelief, and we all waited.

'You will not call,' he said decisively. 'I need your lot for three things. Birth, marriage, and death, and I have two of them over. The druids have too much power in this country as it is.'

Then the penny dropped, and he turned to Barrington, saying: 'You agree, don't you? I liked your speak about that filthy, anti-Christian boycott.' And to Parkinson, in astonishment: 'You're not a druid freak, are you?'

'They only did one of those three things for me,' said Tom, whose father had been head of the longshoremen's union in San Francisco.

The embarrassment had thickened, as we waited for Brendan's next salvo. He had become dimly aware that he might have gone too far, but his way of making up for it was, if anything, worse. He swayed over the cluttered table, surveying us all disapprovingly through lidded, half-drunken eyes.

CHAPTER THREE

'Not that you liberal fuckers have the right to judge priests, anyway. You're nearly as good at the craw-thumping yourselves. As for the fukken French' – turning to my wife – 'everyone knows about them. Even the few poor priests they have left are sex mechanics. You'd never hear the class of thing about Irish priests that you hear about French. They may wear long skirts, but they still chase the judies.'

Then he focused again on the young priest, in case he might have relaxed a little. 'In the name of God, Father, how do you do it?'

The question was rhetorical, and the priest fielded it as best he could, even managing to tell a slightly risqué story himself, about a reformed street walker in his former parish. He began, however, by apologising in advance in case he offended the 'tender ears of Mrs Montague'.

'Tender ears,' cried Brendan incredulously. 'Do you know who you're talking to? Sure, French girls study naked men in school. She could give you a course on sex education. Paris is a bit bigger than Westland Row, you know.'

Parkinson chuckled, but none of us knew what to do about the situation: the young priest was now scarlet, while Brendan remained triumphantly on course, dominating a hushed, partly amused, partly dismayed, and wholly captive audience. Brendan rocked back and forwards, before he attacked again, this time to bring down the curtain. Once more, it was couched as an apology to the priest, but Brendan's commiseration could be more scornful than his dismissal.

'It's all right, this anti-clerical lark, blasting the poor druids for everything. But no matter what Parkinson thinks, or any of our so-called liberal writers say, there's a lot to be said for the Irish clergy. The Irish priest; the flower of the fucking flock, the apple of

God's eye, toiling under the hot sun to save the soul of the black heathen. As a matter of fact, do you know, Father – ' he paused rhetorically, to better focus in on his target, who shifted, smiling uneasily. 'As a matter of fact, statistically speaking, there have been more Irish nuns and priests eaten by cannibals in foreign parts than any other variety.'

Even Brendan couldn't surpass that one. The priest took his leave hurriedly, but the dinner party was past recovery. Parkinson and Barrington moved into the night, talking in low voices, and I recalled a window where we could knock for a drink after closing time. We offered to bring Madeleine, but she had had enough Irishry for one evening.

Brendan and I made our way to the Beehive, and, as the pints were being creamed off, he ventured a sort of apology. 'Did I ruin your evening, John?'

'No,' I said resignedly, 'but, as usual, you drastically changed the script.'

*

In his short obituary in *The Telegraph*, reprinted in *Nonplus*, 'Behan, Master of Language,' Flann O'Brien is both accurate and generous in his analysis of his doomed contemporary:

> There has been no Irishman quite like him and his play-writing, which I personally found in parts crude and offensive as well as entertaining, was only a fraction of a peculiarly complicated personality. He was in face much more a player than a play-wright or, to use a Dublin saying, 'he was as good as a play.' He exuded good nature. He excelled in language and

was a total master of bad language. That latter part of his achievement must remain unknown to the world at large but his personal associates will sorrowfully cherish the memory of it as something unique and occasionally frightening. I have personally never heard the like of it, and it could become enchanting when the glittering scurrilities changed with ease from native Dublinese to good Irish or bookeity French ... It is this sense of ebullience, zest, exuberance, that will remain to tell of Brendan Behan ...

What aspects of his 'peculiarly complicated personality' brought about his downfall? There was his sexual ambiguity, for Brendan was, to use a Dublinism, a 'bicycle', or bisexual, pedalling forlornly with both feet. His first biographer, Ulick O'Connor, made a discreet attempt to raise 'the pubic hare', to use Brendan's own idiom, but Beatrice was still alive, as were his formidable parents, Stephen and Kathleen. Imagine convincing that pair that their chiseller was bent, when even Beatrice, who knew of her husband's proclivities, felt obliged to deny them. Perhaps it was a natural enough consequence of his years in prison, but a married man with an international reputation would have had few opportunities for such specialised adventures.

If Brendan had been more sophisticated, he might have worked out a *modus vivendi*, like many another in the strangely tolerant city of Dublin. A heavily-rouged Micheal MacLiammoir could often be glimpsed sauntering along Baggot Street, yet he and his partner Hilton Edwards were almost pillars of Irish society, with their Gate Theatre irreverently known as 'Sodom' to the Abbey's 'Begorrah'. But Brendan was basically conventional, even in his shock tactics, and the total frankness of a Jean Genet was not for him. Although they had both spent time in prison, Brendan was upset by Genet's autobiography, particularly his attraction to uniforms: 'I could never sink so low as to lick a policeman's boot,' said Brendan disgustedly.

Most of his younger male contemporaries endured the occasional pass from Brendan, if he took a shine to you. But the advance was usually so shy and stumbling as to be easily brushed off: the publicity-hungry Behan, who sought the crowd's applause, was also deeply vulnerable. At the height of his fame, when he was staying in a West End London hotel, he took a fancy to a telegraph boy, who was bringing him messages of congratulation. Brendan was afraid to lay a hand on him, but liked him so much that he began to send telegrams to himself, just in order to see the boy and exchange a few pleasantries.

'I think he liked me,' said Brendan wistfully, 'but if I'd made a move, it could have been all over the papers in the morning.'

For all his impulses in that direction, Brendan seemed reluctant to pass through the mirror, to use Cocteau's image. For, after all, one does not love in a vacuum, and declaring his homosexuality would have entailed a whole change of lifestyle that Brendan ultimately shied from. Or perhaps his real torture was that he was more or less equally attracted to both sexes, an ambivalence which might have been an albatross. Anyway, there can be no doubt that Brendan's sexual ambiguity, with all its attendant confusions, conflicts and guilt, was part of what Flann O'Brien calls 'his peculiarly complicated personality'.

A more recent biographer, Michael O'Sullivan, profits from a much more liberal climate, where homo-eroticism is not a dirty secret, and of course Brendan's parents have since journeyed to the great pub in the sky. But perhaps we are succumbing to a fashionable illusion in attributing most of Brendan's misfortunes to his hobbled emotional and sexual state. It is a factor, certainly, but there is no rule that says that an artist has to be sexually satisfied. It was indulgence, not frustration, that helped to ruin Oscar Wilde, and E.M. Forster's artistic silence coincides with his leaving his mother for a freer life in London and elsewhere. Sublimation, as Freud argues, may indeed be a greater artistic dynamo than gratification.

Then there was Brendan's alcoholism. In his last years, there were all kinds of incidents, some still funny, like his seizing the lapels of a respectable attendant at Smyth's of the Green (a genteel wine shop and delicatessen), and denouncing him as 'a scruff hound, dirt bird, murderer!' But when he appeared in court with dark glasses to conceal bruises sustained when resisting arrest, he seemed like somebody on the downward slope. I found it harder and harder to talk to him when we met, and of course by nightfall he was drunk, and there is a simple human law that no one can survive such punishment for more than two decades. Many reasons can be advanced for his alcoholism: the childlike uncertainty that still showed in his stammer, the violence and thwarted sexuality of his prison days, the tension between his drive towards success and his sympathy with the underdog, and, of course, his Granny English, who introduced him to booze when most of us were making our First Communion. Certainly he bore a heavier psychological burden than most, so that fame became both an excuse and an escape. Besides, he was diagnosed as diabetic, and his liver and kidneys had probably already been damaged by the severe beatings he had received in Walton Gaol. It is eerie to re-read the passage in *Borstal Boy* where he speculates that, 'Maybe this bit of a belting ... would be a contributory cause of my early death in the years to come ...'

If you compare the two accounts of Brendan's release from

borstal in *Borstal Boy*, 1958, and the beginning chapter of *Confessions of an Irish Rebel*, 1965, you can chart the coarsening of sensibility. The first is fresh, restrained, a real writer's voice, for Brendan was, above all, a natural. The second, alas, is full of bluster, the tiresome repetitions of even the most brilliant bar room wag. The later book was dictated and published posthumously, and, though there are wonderful stories in it, pathos has been replaced by pugnacity, a comedian's hectic patter, as though he could not leave a story alone. Despite the objections of some of his harsher critics, however, there is nothing inherently wrong with dictation, which, after all, served Henry James well. And some of the shorter, dictated books, like *Brendan Behan's New York*, are still full of his infectious bonhomie, and do not betray the same lack of focus.

This loss of control was mirrored in his physical deterioration. The young Brendan was a comely, curly-headed lad with small feet and hands; the prematurely aged Behan was a sagging gladiator. Or a sad, stricken bull, dying publicly on its feet. There are accounts by Aidan Higgins in *The Balcony of Europe* and by Cronin in *Dead as Doornails* of Brendan in his last stages; shame on them, they lack both generosity and compassion, although perhaps both writers had feared and faced the same fate for themselves.

For alcoholism has been the fall of many writers, the strict loneliness of the craft compensated for by the easy communion of the pub, bar or café. Parkinson grimly remarked in *The Nation*, in 1957, that he hoped no one would invite Brendan to America to emulate Dylan Thomas. There was even a physical resemblance, though Thomas kept a haunting sense of what he was losing. Hemingway, surprisingly, is a closer comparison, the early war wounds wearing down his bloated body and wearied mind until the association mania of the alcoholic swamped the discipline. Even the

CHAPTER THREE

later, exhausted Joyce of *Finnegans Wake* may not be exempt. As for Berryman's days in Dublin, chanting his *Dream Songs* in the pub ... With the help of David Astor, the editor of the *Observer*, we tried to lure Brendan into a clinic, but treatment for alcoholism was then in its infancy, and Brendan had a horror of being institutionalised.

But I should not leave Brendan on a sour note: he shone like a good deed in the murky world of mid-twentieth century Dublin. He told me once about being briefly locked in the BBC by producers anxious to get a sober performance from him. Bored and restless, he searched for some distraction, and came upon a cache of old-fashioned official rejection slips. Mischievously, he filled them out and addressed them to nearly every Irish writer he knew. So Patrick Kavanagh was thanked for his long poem, *The Bog-Trotter's Funeral*, which 'failed to get off the ground'. Messers (*sic*) O'Connor and O'Faolain, 'c/o the *Bell* Magazine' were thanked 'for your story about an old people's home in Cork, but regrettably it is too gloomily provincial'. Benedict Kiely was thanked 'for submitting your "Tale of Tyrone", which unfortunately we found a shade long-winded'. Whether it happened or not, it was a playful notion, and typical of Brendan in his prime. When he died, another of the most touching obituaries was by his fellow Dubliner, the writer and critic John Jordan, who quoted Shakespeare, 'Boy, bristle thy courage up, for Falstaff he is dead.'

The friendly little bull, dazzled and confused by the glare of publicity, the roar of the crowd, found that the amphitheatre he craved had become a killing ring.

CHAPTER FOUR

LIAM DOLMEN
or
Hell on a Green Isle

I first heard of Liam Miller through an O'Meara cousin of mine from Longford, who was attending night classes at the National College of Art, and staying in a digs in Dublin run by, I think, a Polish lady. He said that there was a very artistic young fellow from the Irish Midlands who was staying in the same digs and studying architecture, called Bill or William Miller.

When I met my future publisher at his basement offices in Upper Mount Street in 1956, he was definitely Liam, not Bill or William. An intense, dark-avised figure, he looked Jewish, or at least Eastern European, a pale unworldly scholar from another time and place, who had perhaps found refuge in Ireland. It was a time when scholars, like the palaeographer Ludwig Bieler, found a haven in places like Dublin's Institute for Advanced Studies, and Liam Miller seemed as exotic a savant as any of them.

In fact, he was a butcher's son from Mountrath in County Laois who had just founded a publishing house, and was dedicated to Irish poetry and drama in a way that had not been seen in Dublin since the early days of the Irish Literary Renaissance, the era of the Cuala Press and Maunsel and Roberts. In order to subsidise his ideal, Liam was also a job printer who took on most of the work that came his way. I did not observe him at the very beginning of his career, since I had embarked on my Grand Tour of America, but I had already heard positive reports of his dedication. It seemed he had discovered his vocation when he bought a small hand press, and fell in love with the lovely process of printing; years later he would describe, with a chuckle, how marvellously erotic the technical language of the trade was. And his growing sense of design probably came from his architectural training.

A literary or artistic movement is usually the conjunction of several talents into a constellation at the same time and place. And the foundation of the Dolmen Press coincided with the diffident first steps of Richard Murphy (*The Archaeology of Love*), Thomas Kinsella (*Poems*, and *Another September*) and myself (*Forms of Exile*), in the mid- to late 1950s. I remember a little congregation of us outside the basement press, and someone saying: 'Not a bad place to become the centre of Irish literature!' In fact it was an infant enterprise, and Liam was learning as he went along, so that the sour comments of Philip Larkin on his rejection were only partly justified. He refers in his letters to the Dolmen Press as a 'chicken-hearted institution', as indeed it was in the sense of age, slightly cocksure, without yet being a fully-grown Pathé rooster crowing its wares.

Since we lived around the corner from each other, it was natural that we should begin to work together. Indeed, we were so close by that I could judge Liam's mood by the hour he went down to the press, as well as his general gait of going, dark head up or down, briefcase borne lightly or like a load of lead. I understood his problems, trying to subsidise a small poetry press while supporting a young family, and while I still had no children myself, I was sympathetic to his cares. But when he delayed publication of my first manuscript, I realised that his financial state was chronically constrained, and agreed to contribute to its appearance in 1958 with a donation of £40. It was nearly three weeks' salary in those days, but I was nearing the advanced age of thirty, with poems all over the place, though no individual volume to my name.

I think that this may have helped to create an unease, an imbalance, in our financial relationship. And may also have led to my partly leaving Dolmen for MacGibbon and Kee, when Timothy O'Keefe offered me my first real advance for *Poisoned Lands*. In the long run, I don't regret this move, because it gave me an influence on their Irish list, as a first reader, from Anthony West's prose to Kavanagh's poetry. And another advance helped me to work on my short story collection, *Death of a Chieftain*. While Timothy O'Keefe had only a poor sense of the minutely complex world of poetry politics, he did his best by the stories, and for a young man intent on making a career as a writer, having an English publisher seemed a positive move.

But of course I never really left Liam, who had become a good friend, and whose creative generosity outweighed his financial uncertainties. We worked together on what was to become *The Dolmen Miscellany*, the first anthology of the then new Irish writing; I had an amused letter from Aidan Higgins about descending into the basement with his proofs and being impressed by the amount of beard he found there. And of course there was the private publication of my poem, *Like Dolmens Round my Childhood, the Old People*, in 1960, after it had received a prize in Belfast. I have often wondered whether our obsession with standing stones was mutual, or was mine sparked off unconsciously by the name of his press. Or, more likely, the new interest in archaeology in Ireland, which I would satirise in the title story of *Death of a Chieftain*. Our

CHAPTER FOUR

second personal collaboration was with my sequence of love poems, *All Legendary Obstacles* (1966), which came out at roughly the same time as Kinsella's *Wormwood,* as a Dolmen Edition. (Since I had recently edited the collected poems of Patrick Kavanagh, I was eager that Irish poetry should move from the peat to the private, especially since our country was rapidly changing, with the cities burgeoning and factory farming replacing the old rural ways.) I was very close to the painter Barrie Cooke at the time, though I am still startled by his sprawling cover design, which caused Tom Kinsella no end of mirth. He wanted to know how I thought poetry was being served by having a distinguished Irish history professor copulating on the cover. Like a Rorschach blot, the inky incoherence of the design laid itself open to many interpretations.

So when I came back from Paris to Dublin for editorial sessions, or Claddagh meetings, I would often stay with Jo and Liam in their house in 94 Lower Baggot Street. It was a splendid bohemian haven where all seemed welcome, singers like Ronnie Drew (I think he met his wife there), actors like Eamonn Keane, playwright John B.'s mischievous brother. Whatever the Millers had, they shared, with a joint (of meat) coming up from Mountrath at the weekend, and the kettle always on the boil. And occasionally they held parties, where I met a heroine of our childhood, Patricia Lynch, whose story, *The Turf Cutter's Donkey,* was in every Irish household, and who was accompanied by a bright young journalist Mary Holland. The editorial sessions were held in that front room caught by Cartier-Bresson, with Tom Kinsella and myself sharing eager plans, which a benevolent bearded Liam sought to orchestrate. It was a fascinating three-way dialogue among equals, and when Liam struck a financial rock in the mid-1960s, we were able to organise a rescue committee, which met in that same room.

So when I came to publish *A Chosen Light* (MacGibbon and Kee, 1967), I dedicated it to Liam and Garech Browne, whom I describe as 'friendly hosts', in the double sense of hospitality, and soldiers in the service of a new Irish aesthetic. And Liam and I had begun our most important collaboration, the publication of sections of *The Rough Field*. This was the kind of task he loved, finding a format for 'Patriotic Suite' (1966), which was partly a riposte to the overly nationalistic celebrations of that year. Hence the green cover with a Derricke illustration that Kinsella rightly saw as a parody of 'Reidy's Band', Sean Ó Riada's motley crew of traditional musicians in his *Ceolteori Chullainn*. After the liturgical format of 'The Bread God', which embarrassed most Irish reviewers, came 'Hymn to the New Omagh Road' with its look of an old-fashioned accounting ledger. Perhaps too old-fashioned, so Liam replaced it with the open postcard format of 'A New Siege'. As these individual pamphlets appeared, I found myself going back to the North more and more, compelled by the burgeoning of the long poem, which reflected a new political restiveness.

To work on a text with Liam was fascinating, a kind of intellectual dance. He experimented with various typefaces, lengths of page, and quality of paper, always inviting comment, seeking an ideal blend or marriage of the visual and the verbal. All those sections of *The Rough Field* are now collector's items, as is the first edition of the complete book. I cannot imagine anyone else responding so eagerly to the challenge of an unusual text, balancing the talents of both editor and publisher. I think that period may well be the apogee of Liam's achievement, when he was planning Kinsella's *Tain*, and helping me plough *The Rough Field*.

Ironically, during what now seem to me the halcyon years of the Dolmen Press, both Kinsella and I were living mainly out of the country, Tom in Carbondale, Illinois, or later Philadelphia, and me in Paris or 'improbable California'. 'Life in Ireland without you and Tom,' wrote Liam, 'is hell on a green isle.' But these lengthy absences seemed to make our partnership with him prosper, so that when we did meet, it was with the intensity and enthusiasm of real colleagues re-finding one other. In late 1970, or early 1971, Liam prompted me gently, 'Maybe you should begin to draw this long poem in. It can't go on forever, and every farmer needs a harvest.'

But I leap ahead. My friend Timothy O'Keefe had lost his battle to preserve MacGibbon and Kee as an independent and creative publisher, and had been swallowed by Bernstein of Granada. So with *Tides* (1970), I had officially returned to Dolmen (Kinsella declared tartly that I should never have left). When Liam was on a visit to Paris to meet Beckett, I had introduced him to Bill Hayter, the engraver and printer, for whom I had done a sequence called 'Sea Changes'. They got along famously because both were demons for work, and Liam commissioned him to do a cover for *Tides*, with a female form swirling through water. My personal life was changing at the time, and I remember the excitement of working with Liam on the proofs in the old Majestic Hotel in Fitzwilliam Street, where Berryman had begun his Dublin stay, at my suggestion. Poet and mystic Robin Skelton was there, the artist Jack Coughlin from Montague, Massachusetts, and the young woman who would become my second wife. We were all in high good humour, and that combination of hard work and hijinks was characteristic of almost all my dealings with Liam Dolmen.

Sometimes we met after work in Phil Ryan's pub in Baggot Street, now absorbed into the fashionably bleak façade of Ronnie Tallon's Bank of Ireland, further diluting Dublin's Georgian heritage. It was a comfortable upper room, with a view across the street, a favourite watering hole for distinguished older writers like Kate O'Brien and Patrick Kavanagh, as well as some of the stray McDaid's young, hopefully plying Liam with manuscripts. For after Kinsella, Murphy and myself, there was another generation, people like the melancholy James McAuley, and the always exuberant James Liddy who was editing *Arena,* which fostered the post-*Collected* Kavanagh and printed an illustrated version of my *The Siege of Mullingar.* If the family were away, Liam liked nothing better than a brief descent into the whirlpool of McDaid's itself. There was Kavanagh in his corner, coughing and snorting, Myles hunched over his whiskey before heading abruptly home, the artist Sean O'Sullivan discoursing in French, and, of course, the Rathmines brigade, Pearse Hutchinson, the poet, and John Jordan, editor of *Poetry Ireland.* Leaning over John, trying to comprehend some intensely muttered intellectual message, a warm torrent of sour-smelling stout suddenly flowed over my head. Turning in astonishment, I confronted a beaming Liam.

'You are John,' he explained with lunatic logic. 'And you are standing by Jordan.'

Liam also did his best to help our older writers, introducing the later Austin Clarke to a larger audience, and organising celebrations for his seventieth birthday, including a small *festschrift* with contributions by Ted Hughes, Christopher Ricks, Charles Tomlinson, Serge Fauchereau, as well as the usual Irish suspects. There was a launch in a Baggot Street bar with the unfortunate name The Crooked Bawbee (or 'Bent Coin'), where I made a clumsy speech in French and English, which brought the wrath of Padraic Colum down on my head. I had referred to his longevity, since he was eighty-five at the time, and he said tartly that a poet's age was irrelevant to the merits of his poetry.

And Liam tried to be friendly with Kavanagh, who, after all, lived

CHAPTER FOUR

only up the way in Pembroke Road, but the other Old Master could be very irascible. Although once, when Liam was on his own, we brought back Kavanagh from the pub for a rest and a feed of bacon, sausage and eggs. I had just visited a doctor friend of mine who, when I was sleepless or despondent, would offer me samples from his medicine cupboard. One tablet made me feel particularly lively, and I asked the morose Kavanagh if he would like to try them.

'Only take one,' I cautioned. 'They're very strong.'

Patrick returned to the pub, and swallowed the entire contents of the phial with compulsive fervour, washing it down with whatever drinks were going.

Next morning he was banging on Liam's door.

'Have you more of that stuff?' he pleaded. 'I loved it! I took off like a rocket!'

Unfortunately, a dispute sprang up between him and Liam, who was publishing a small edition of the text of Patrick's television *Self Portrait*, which had introduced the poet to a larger, more popular audience. Liam wanted to use some unbuttoned pictures of the poet sprawling or walking around his favourite haunt, Baggot Street Bridge, but Patrick was very sensitive about his dignity as a senior poet, especially now that some belated fame had come to him. He hated to be called 'Paddy' because of the stage Irish implications, and he felt that a book cover showing him in cap and braces would perpetuate the unfortunate early impression of him as a 'rural bard'. So a new cover had to be found, but he remained suspicious of Liam's good intentions.

More even than most publishers, Liam liked to be part of the action, and to meet his writers socially, which of course worked to the advantage of those who lived in Dublin and could ease his solitary dedication with pleasant pub sessions. His brother-in-law,

LIAM DOLMEN

Liam Browne, dealt mainly with the commercial side of the business, leaving Miller largely free to focus on the editorial side. But I don't think he ever set up a proper mechanism for dealing with submissions, so it was into this trough that Seamus Heaney's early manuscript, *An Advancement of Learning*, fell. Very few people in Dublin, apart from myself, had yet heard of Heaney; Tom Kinsella was away in America and my visits back were as irregular as inspiration. As for Liam, he could not attach a face to the name, and certainly never mentioned it to me, or, I believe, Tom. Not knowing of this early manuscript, I recommended Heaney to O'Keefe at MacGibbon and Kee, but by that time Faber and Faber had already snapped him up. It is interesting to speculate how his career would have developed if Liam had had the good sense to ask my advice about this promising young voice from the North, but then Belfast, and the North generally, had not yet swung back into the Southern consciousness.

For Liam and most of his Dublin contemporaries, the North of Ireland barely existed except as a distant, thorny place. Even the published sections of *The Rough Field* could not persuade Liam that the North might foster other voices. I suppose that some of this had to do with Dublin's flickering new energy. From a moribund post-'Emergency' city, where dispirited poets drank in murky pubs, it was becoming artistically alive, with Liam as one of its leading lights. The last thing Southerners wanted in that new climate was to consider the unresolved 'Northern problem', which had been, by general unspoken consent, moved to the back burner. So the rejection of Seamus was a missed opportunity, with myself and Tom both out of the country, and Liam overwhelmed.

When I finally gathered in *The Rough Field*, at Liam's behest (I had some vague plan of basing it on the thirteen months of the Old

Year), we set out to find a visual equivalent. The opening section, 'Home Again' was also published separately, with a line drawing of the cauldron from County Tyrone in the National Museum, as a symbol of the prodigal's return. And we cast around for similar emblems for each section, but other images did not come so readily to hand. Nor did the idea of putting the already published sections together, with their varying typefaces and design, seem to work; instead of indicating the diversity of voices in the text, it looked like a typographical jumble. Then Liam triumphantly reproduced the Derricke engravings (one of which we had already used for 'Patriotic Suite'), which underlined the dialogue between present and past that is at the heart of the work. And the unusually large dimensions of the first edition was part of the effect, a blend of ledger and missal. Those engravings and broad dimensions were already associated with me, since they had also been used for the pamphlet of 'The Planter and the Gael' tour of the North, featuring myself as Gael and John Hewitt as Planter. But that slowly growing English institution, the Poetry Book Society, did not even give it a Recommendation: perhaps, like the Australian poet Peter Porter, they detected what they considered a latent republicanism, failing to realise that the book is woven of many strands, including the psychic defeat of my patriot father.

Besides, I did not fulfil their new expectations of an Irish poet – expectations that I, by helping to revive Kavanagh, had unwittingly encouraged. While celebrating Patrick's country themes and imagery, I had hoped that succeeding Irish poets would move on, embracing personal, urban and indeed international subjects, as Patrick had tried to do himself. It did not occur to me that Kavanagh's rural themes would harden into a formula, to which a new generation would be expected to hew.

A further dimension was added to *The Rough Field* when Paddy Moloney arranged the traditional music implicit in the text for a public performance, first in the Peacock Theatre in Dublin, and then in London, at the Roundhouse in Chalk Farm, which was recorded for Claddagh Records. Again, Liam helped to produce the dramatic version, and clearly enjoyed the task, working with a medley of actors like Pat Magee and Alun Owen, and writers like Benedict Kiely, Seamus Heaney and myself. For the theatre was another love of his, and his work in The Lantern, the basement theatre underneath the British Embassy in Merrion Square, was part of his fertile vision. Great publishers have a kind of diverse energy, and Liam was a sort of Dublin Diaghilev during the 1960s and 1970s, coaxing and arranging things into existence. I brought over a small shoal of French poets, like Michel Deguy, and it was under the light of The Lantern that John Berryman gave the only public reading of his Dublin *hegira*.

When we met in Dublin in the 1960s, I was either coming from Paris, or going to California, and our meetings had an almost hectic quality, but after I returned to Ireland in the 1970s we met more easily and often. *A Slow Dance* (1975) was followed by a reclaimed *Poisoned Lands* (1976) and *The Great Cloak* (1978). What Liam had restored for poets like Kinsella and myself was the possibility of having a normal career, one volume evolving from another. But with *Selected Poems* (1982), and, more particularly, *The Dead Kingdom* (1984), I began to realise that something was wrong. Liam did not bring his old enthusiasm to planning my new books. Indeed he farmed out the *Selected Poems* to my Canadian editor, Barry Callaghan; I had the impression that it was not only because he was older, but also because he was distracted. Or perhaps my work was now too familiar to him: he was very excited by working with

CHAPTER FOUR

English poet Kathleen Raine on her books of lyrics. And above all, her extraordinary study of the esoteric side of Yeats, *Yeats the Initiate*, which, with its many illustrations, must have been one of the most expensive of all the Dolmen productions. While sustaining the new poetry, Liam had always been a Yeatsian, and this opulent volume was his deepest homage to that mighty presence, as seen by Kathleen, friend of Mrs Yeats and a poetic initiate herself.

When it came to *The Dead Kingdom*, I found most of the images for the five movements myself, in sharp contrast to our exuberant collaboration on the illustrations for *The Rough Field*. He accepted them gladly, but the old gleam was gone, and when the book appeared, it had shrunk in format, as though he had had to economise on paper. Only the Canadian publication, from Callaghan's Exile Editions, restored the larger dimensions that we had envisaged. And Barry, a bit of a Diaghilev himself in his efforts to warm Canada's frozen wastes, warned me that he feared my old friend Liam was 'losing it'.

Some of Liam's distractions were indeed financial. It was almost impossible then to run a small prestigious poetry press with high literary standards but little or no commercial clout. Liam was wonderful at designing a book, but when the child was delivered he was often less interested, although arranging co-publication could still bring zest to his eye and step. We had all spent a hilarious semi-holiday at a Celtic festival in Toronto, Tom Kinsella and myself reading, and Seán Ó Riada playing. Liam helped to produce an offbeat and ultra-modern version of Yeats's play, *The Only Jealousy of Emer*, with designs by a Canadian Jewish sculptor called Sorel Etrog, who dressed Cuchulain as an American college football star, bulky shoulder pads and all. Liam published the proceedings (including a clash between me and Conor Cruise O'Brien on the subject of the North), in a bumper volume called *The Celtic Consciousness*. I accidentally met him on Fifth Avenue after he had sold this blockbuster to a New York publisher, George Braziller, and he was high as a kite, playful as a kitten. And of course he had established a good working relationship with Oxford, Dillon Johnston's Wake Forest University Press, and sometimes Barry Callaghan of Canada's Exile Editions. By now he was recognised as the founding father of modern Irish publishing, and he would meet his younger confreres, like Seamus Cashman of Wolfhound and Anne Tannahill of Blackstaff, for convivial evenings at the Frankfurt Book Fair.

I wonder sometimes if I played my part in his problems by not insisting on a proper author-publisher relationship; I knew little or nothing about the details of these four-way publications. It may shock people to learn that I never received royalties, even for *The Rough Field*, but we operated under a kind of gentleman's agreement: he produced the Book Beautiful, and I could have as many copies as I wanted whenever I needed them. I usually had another salary from teaching, which he patently did not, so why worry? A few times I tried to work out how matters stood, but the figures varied so wildly that I gave up trying to make sense of it all. The only aspect of this haphazard book-keeping that made me a little sore was when the press absorbed royalties from re-publication as their due. But it is hard to dun a generous friend over money matters, and Liam had become more taciturn, so that I could not mount the rescue operation I had tried in the mid-1960s, when he was in trouble.

Besides, I had experienced, in a minor way, some of the pressures he was under. In the 1970s, I tried to operate a private imprint, the Golden Stone, to maintain a friendly rivalry with Kinsella's Peppercannister, and to generally keep the juices flowing in a then artistically sleepy Cork. Liam was, as ever, helpful with the planning and design, but it became clear, by the third publication, that we did not have the kind of follow-through to keep such an enterprise going. It did, however, give me a sense of how much dedication is required to keep even a minuscule imprint alive. All the tedious details of packaging and posting, lists of review and complimentary copies to journals and libraries, maintaining clear accounts, handling readers' enthusiasms and rages: it wasn't long before I lost heart. There were also local difficulties; I could not find someone to bind the special editions, and the then president of University College, Cork, feared that I was running a lucrative commercial operation from my office in the English Department, which was the only stable address we then had.

I was also realising that I did not possess the publisher's temperament. It takes a certain kind of obsessive passion to corral and organise a number of writers, to encourage their gift, edit their poetry or prose, all the while keeping in sight the ideals of one's own particular publishing house. I have already mentioned Diaghilev, and indeed an impresario quality seems to be needed. At best, this quality fosters talent and creates lovely books. But it has its dark side as well, as when Dolmen felt no urgency to pay royalties, or absorbed authors' cheques into their own coffers: sometimes the imprint is seen as greater than the authors it serves.

The bond between author and publisher is rarely analysed, yet it is an essential and often emotional relationship, especially when the material being edited and published is creative. Timothy O'Keefe would use my arrival in London as an excuse for a lunch at the Spanish Club, drinking clubs all afternoon, and Museum Street's

Plough in the evening. And although there would not be all that much direct conversation about work, it would be a consistent undercurrent. Liam was the same, and during those hours of comradeship, there did not seem to be a mean bone in his body. He wrote to me about my part in Kavanagh's *Collected Poems*, saying it would re-establish him in the race (like a lot of Irish people, he was fond of racing terms). And he echoed Behan's favourite war-cry, 'Hump the begrudgers!'

Liam Miller's end was hard. He had established a new rhythm with the press on the North Side of Dublin, and his home in a former rectory in Mountrath, his home town, with the river flowing at the end of the garden, and the Goldsmithian peace of those Midland fields. And yet something *was* wrong. He was slower and more troubled: he had a fine room that served as his office with many of his precious icons around (mainly books and engravings), and we worked there on our last project, my selected essays, a large volume of nearly three hundred pages. I remember him being particularly vehement about wishing to include many of the sleeve notes I had done for Claddagh Records, on Graves, Sidney Goodsir Smith and of course the now neglected Ambassador Iremonger. I was never to see that manuscript again. And when I adjourned to the local, as usual, his daughter accompanied me, but Liam excused himself on the grounds of fatigue.

When I next saw Liam alone, he was in Baggot Street hospital, and the prognosis was not good. He was trying to keep the flag flying, however, sipping whiskey as he enthused about his latest project, an edition of *Dubliners* illustrated by Louis le Brocquy, a project which would later be taken from him when he was too enfeebled to see it through. His daughter Maire was trying to run the press, and had published some of my students, the younger Cork poets Sean Dunne and Greg Delanty, a link Liam had already forged when he published Thomas McCarthy. While I was there, a meal came, and I was impressed by the zest with which Liam tackled his grub: this was not a man resigned to illness.

All through his downward spiral, his fortitude was remarkable. Even to the last, he loved the friendly jar, but a growing despair underlay everything. Lying in a relative's home in the North Side, after being discharged from hospital, he showed me the swellings on his body, and declared grimly, 'I don't think even the poet's blessing could banish these.' And yet he prayed, and believed, all the more when he was removed to a hospice in South Dublin. What characterised Liam for me, above all, was his profound Christianity. Indeed, he seems to me to have been a medieval man, in his devotion to printing as a craft, and in his faith, which was being so sorely tested. I think he was rarely as happy as when he worked with the Vatican, designing a Missal for the English-speaking world, or presenting a volume to the present Pope. A photo shows Liam, lean and bearded, exchanging smiles with the burly John Paul.

At his funeral, as Tom Kinsella spoke, I could not but notice the contrast between Liam's fate and that of most of his family, who were long-lived, as the tombstone told. As the mourners scattered back to Dublin, there were many casualties: the singer Ronnie Drew was very upset, and I was not so far behind myself. Rumour had it that Liam had died in debt, but then, in his precarious position as a pioneer of Irish publishing, he had been moving in and out of solvency all his working life, always bouncing back – until now.

I was able to do one last service for my old friend, because I was friendly, at the time, with the librarian in charge of the Special Collections at Wake Forest University. I suggested that he should consider Liam's archive, rich with lively correspondence, and offering intriguing glimpses into the process, mechanics and day-to-day working life of a whole literary period, which he had helped to orchestrate. And of course, as I hope this testimony proves, Liam's presence is still with many of us. His wife Josephine described to me how, sifting through his papers and books, she had the impression of being guided, her hand opening just the right book at the right moment. When I called on his sister in Mountrath, not far from their own old home, she told me that she was sure that Liam was in heaven, and that she prayed to him. If he is, he is probably ensconced in a corner with a small printing press, and starting out all over again.

CHAPTER FIVE

CLADDAGH RAGA

This is a little like an Evelyn Waugh story, a great deal of fun, with an underlying seriousness, even sorrow. It begins with my meeting Garech Browne, who was walking along Herbert Street with Brendan Behan. Before glimpsing him, I heard his haughty, port wine voice – a voice that resonated with Ascendancy privilege – which instantly got my Gaelic hackles up. But I was gradually forced to realise that underneath that straw-coloured thatch, and behind that Lord Snooty baby face, lay a real if untrained intellect, and considerable staying power.

He wanted to form a record company, which could have been regarded as the whim of a wealthy young man, but was actually deeply serious. Even before he came of age, Garech had a growing knowledge of Irish traditional music, going so far as to study Irish and take lessons in the *uilleann* pipes, or what Shakespeare calls the 'woollen' or 'elbow pipes'. A painting by Edward Maguire shows a young, earnest Garech, with those plump schoolboy cheeks, squeezing that intricate instrument. And, to my greater surprise, he was interested in recording writers as well. We decided to start a Spoken Word series, and agreed about the older writers we admired, whose voices we wished to capture reading their own work, although it was hard to imagine the likes of Hugh MacDiarmid and Patrick Kavanagh in a modern recording studio. But with his curious mixture of diplomacy and determination, Garech managed to persuade most, even the more grumpy and belligerent, like Liam O'Flaherty, whom he had been eager to record for a long time since they both came from the West. And Garech's father, Dominick, Lord Oranmore and Browne, had been friends with him.

But back to the founding of Claddagh Records, that Mad Hatter's venture. As I have mentioned, Garech rang me up one day, asking if he could borrow my wife, because his then-girlfriend wanted to go to Sybil Connolly's fashion show in Merrion Square. Since it was one of the major social events of the Season, the press were bound to attend, and he feared that they would gleefully fasten on his association with his young friend, who also happened to be his mother's chambermaid. He needed a decoy, and Madeleine agreed to go along with the scheme, so much so that the confused journalists photographed her instead of Garech's young woman. An article appeared in an early edition of the *Daily Express* with the caption, 'Garech Browne and his Girlfriend Show up for the Fashions' beneath a photo of a smiling Garech and Madeleine strolling side by side. The newspaper realised their mistake and withdrew the edition, but there were enough copies around for us, the outraged husband and his indignant wife, to launch a successful little libel action. On the principle of *noblesse oblige*, I thought that some of the resulting spoils should go into the company, and so we got started.

After late boozy nights with Brendan in the murky Brazen Head, and sessions with Garech in the dim-lit Piper's Club, we finally decided on our first record, *The King of the Pipers*, by Leo Rowsome, the virtuoso piper who had given Garech his early lessons. With the help of my distinguished publisher, Liam Miller – who knew as much about record album covers as we did – we produced a sleeve that shows Leo playing with a wash of colour superimposed over him. In other words, it was supposed to be a two-colour job, but the colours did not take. An amateurish outcome in terms of the look of the thing, but a musical success: the first full-length LP of a traditional Irish piper.

Garech had the musical erudition and I had a typewriter, so we could bang out fairly good sleeve notes together, as we did for Leo Rowsome, and also for our first Spoken Word record, *Almost Everything* by Patrick Kavanagh. Only our text drew a howl of fury from Patrick, who was not even on growling terms with me at the time, since I had helped to produce his *Collected Poems* 'behind his back' and could, therefore, do no good in his eyes. Assisting other writers was not something Patrick understood, since he always suspected an ulterior motive. And Garech and I, in our new capacity as record producers, were learning that some writers could not understand that producing records was different from producing a book: imagine me bickering with my old pal Tom Kinsella over the look of his record cover! I tried to explain that a record cover was a larger canvas than a book, and required bolder visual effects, but he argued that no one would buy a record because of the look of it. And many people had begun to presume that making records was bound to be big business, as though Garech and I were now music industry moguls, when in fact the Spoken Word series invariably lost rather than made money, except for Beckett and Kavanagh.

Claddagh Records was launched at Garech's mews flat in Quinn's Lane, with a firkin of Guinness' porter (of course) in the corner, and a party that roared on until dawn, the first of many such sprawling, splendid parties. The secret of their success was, I think, their mixture of social classes and talents, a heady brew in addition to the Guinness. It was extraordinary: an upper-class Anglo-Irishman with

CHAPTER FIVE

a passion for Irish traditional music, a number of fairly prominent writers including Brendan Behan and Tom Kinsella (who would belie his sombre appearance by bursting into song), painters and sculptors like Eddie Maguire and Eddie Delaney, and, invariably, an abundance of talented musicians, including the future Chieftains, who were soon to become world famous. Seamus Kelly, drama critic for the *Irish Times*, left that first Claddagh party to write a condescending notice, then returned to plunge back into the hospitality. When I reproached him in Grafton Street for his smart-alec review, he cried incredulously, 'By God, you and Browne *are* serious!'

Austin Clarke provided one of our more memorable Spoken Word albums, but he had been used to recording for the sedate audience of Radio Eireann, so he omitted an orgiastic passage from 'Beyond the Pale', about the dark loves of Dame Kyttler, the Kilkenny witch, and her companion Petronella, who was kissed: 'Introrsely by Black Fitzjames, knighted in hell. / He picked her keyhole with his skeleton, / Fire-freezing through her pelvis…'

Garech and I insisted that it go back in.

'These young people,' Austin marvelled, 'want to hear everything!'

Memories begin to crowd in. I picture the radiant face and abundant red hair of Dolly MacMahon, as she sings 'The Lass of Aughrim', the song sung by Michael Furey in Joyce's 'The Dead'. And Dolly herself was a Furey from Galway, which made her rendition all the more moving. She could be full of mischief as well, as when she persuaded me to warble awkwardly in what was then Dublin's only singing pub, before refusing to sing at all herself. Now the night is clamorous with singing pubs, but Dolly's haunting voice echoes on and on, thanks to that Claddagh record.

The great gift of Máire Áine was as profound as Portuguese *fado* or Spanish *flamenco*. She was the custodian of the ancient *sean nós* tradition, and no one who had heard her harsh, powerful voice could forget it. But she had never recorded that voice, nor even sung on the radio; only Garech was able to lure her onto record, clasping her hand in grave sympathy while she sang one of the most esoteric of Ireland's secret songs, 'Úna Bhán'. Her album, designed by Louis le Brocquy, is called *Tears from a Cliff (Deora Aille)*, a suitable way to describe that voice, strong as flint but charged with pathos.

Garech, as always, was a stickler for detail. Máire Áine's and many another's records became as complex a production as a scholarly article, with bi- or even trilingual record sleeves. How often, late at night when I felt ready for nothing but sleep, would Garech force me to translate Carolan's last words or Bach's German. Relentlessly coaxing, Garech gave the information and demanded the result. Neither my Irish nor my German is really first class, which meant that I had to scour the dictionaries and make sudden phone calls to experts, but Garech insisted on perfection and style, so that many of the Claddagh sleeve notes are richly detailed bibliographical items as well.

The composer Sean Ó Riada, Paddy Moloney, the other Chieftains: I met them all through Garech. I was seduced by the passionate seriousness of Sean Ó Riada, and Garech and I agreed that the public had a partly incomplete view of him, pleased by his orchestral arrangements of old Irish music, but unaware of his own creative achievement. We attempted to redress that by recording Sean's *Hercules Dux Ferrariae*, his first symphonic work, and I never saw him so happy as after that session in London, although he was already growing frail from years of very heavy drinking.

And the exuberant whistle of Paddy Moloney accompanied us everywhere, through Scotland and the Orkneys, or bundled into a

CHAPTER FIVE

London taxi with Robert Graves. Scotland because we had begun a Spoken Word Series on Scots poets. I remember the night Garech and I met them all in an Edinburgh flat. I was pleased to hold my own amongst that formidable, whisky-gulping group of bards, like MacDiarmid and MacCaig. In fact, I saw them all down, except our now-dead host, Sidney Goodsir Smith. But when we got back to our hotel, my self-satisfaction was dealt a low blow. Somehow I had got caught in the revolving door, and was spilled out onto the carpet of the foyer on my hands and knees. 'Good dog,' soothed the night porter, as he guided me to my room. It seemed that he had been a bat man of Churchill's, and so was not unused to such behaviour. Scotland was a splendid adventure, although our manager, Paddy Moloney, sometimes wondered if the sky was raining Scottish poets.

Speaking of Paddy and the Chieftains, on a night when Paddy and the members of his group were drinking with us in Quinn's Lane, we began to wonder what they should be called. 'The Quare Fellas' was considered, then abandoned, doubtless a lucky decision since the word 'queer' would soon change meaning. It happened that I had just finished a long story, 'Death of a Chieftain'. The central character is an upper class Protestant eccentric who hungers for native Irish culture, indeed becomes addicted to it, with unexpected consequences. (I wonder if I might have modelled him on a certain Anglo-Irish Gael of my acquaintance?) Paddy and the boys liked this rather wild, experimental story with its unusual hero, and so 'The Chieftains' were christened, and now they are known from Sydney to San Francisco, Okinawa to the Great Wall of China.

Traditional music has burgeoned now, and might actually be in *too* healthy a state. I sometimes wonder if it is not in danger of being *fleadh*-ed to death, a new torture, with a captive audience banged by *bodhrans* (the Irish tambourine), and pummelled by pipes. Claddagh's original concern was to preserve 'the pure drop', for great musicians, like great poets, are mortal. So as well as preserving the cavernous voice of Patrick Kavanagh, the lugubrious cadences of Austin Clarke, and the strong Scots burr of Hugh MacDiarmid, we have the splendid fiddling of Denis Murphy and his sister Julia, and the piping of Leo Rowsome and Willy Clancy, the singing of Maire Aine, and the Keane sisters whose voices were like the whispering of stones in a riverbed. With the tradition so defined and clarified, new departures become possible. Our crusade for the preservation of Irish music could be compared with the influential early recordings of American jazz and blues. The rich, bittersweet voices of Robert Johnson, Big Bill Bronzy, John Lee Hooker and others would have died with them if they had not been recorded, but because they were preserved, they became the foundation on which modern jazz has grown and flourished, as modern Irish music has also, because of those early recordings.

And we had great fun along the way. The organisers of the early *fleadhanna*, or music festivals, seemed to choose the most boring towns in Ireland for their annual celebrations. I stood on the main street of Mullingar with a stolid citizen as the young poured in for the Whitsun weekend of 1963. Many of the young men, on foot, scooter or roaring motor bicycle, were stripped to the waist, and their 'motts', or girlfriends, were not far behind, with loosened hair and tight jeans.

It was an exhilarating sight, young Ireland on the march towards pleasure, but not to my ageing companion: 'Where under God did that mob come from?'

Splendid weather, splendid music, left us all honeyed with happiness. A cluster of pup tents mushroomed by the Canal, and as I strolled by in the evening, I imitated the heavy tones of a local garda,

CHAPTER FIVE

or old-fashioned parish priest, the kind who flushed lovers out of the ditch with a thump of his blackthorn: 'There's a queer class of unchristian thing going on in there, so remember to say your prayers.'

From every tent came a volley of friendly oaths: 'Fuck off, Father!' Ireland's future had arrived.

> At the Fleadh Cheoil in Mullingar
> There were two sounds, the breaking
> Of glass, and the background pulse
> Of music. Young girls roamed
> The streets with eager faces,
> Shoving for men. Bottles in
> Hand, they rowed out a song:
> *Puritan Ireland's dead and gone,*
> *A myth of O'Connor and O'Faolain.*

The town was jam-packed, yet the great piper, Seamus Ennis, said he would find us a billet, but that I should keep my mouth shut. To my astonishment, buttoning his long black coat, and smoothing his dark hair, he disappeared into the leading hotel, to emerge with a beaming and bowing Manager. We were escorted to the largest set of rooms, the Bridal Suite. What magic had the dark, dignified piper worked?

'Call room service for double brandies, and the bill, and you'll understand,' Seamus chortled.

As we savoured the amber liquid, I discovered that my name had received a lordly prefix (which also explained my complicity with my grinning manservant, since the real Lord Montague had recently been caught in fraught circumstances).

A Touch of the Poet?
The newly married
author at 27, in 1956

Sheba and Solomon:
Yeats and his wife

Madeleine on the beach: 'An Occasion of Sin'

Madeleine flanked by Doris Lessing and
Clancy Sigal

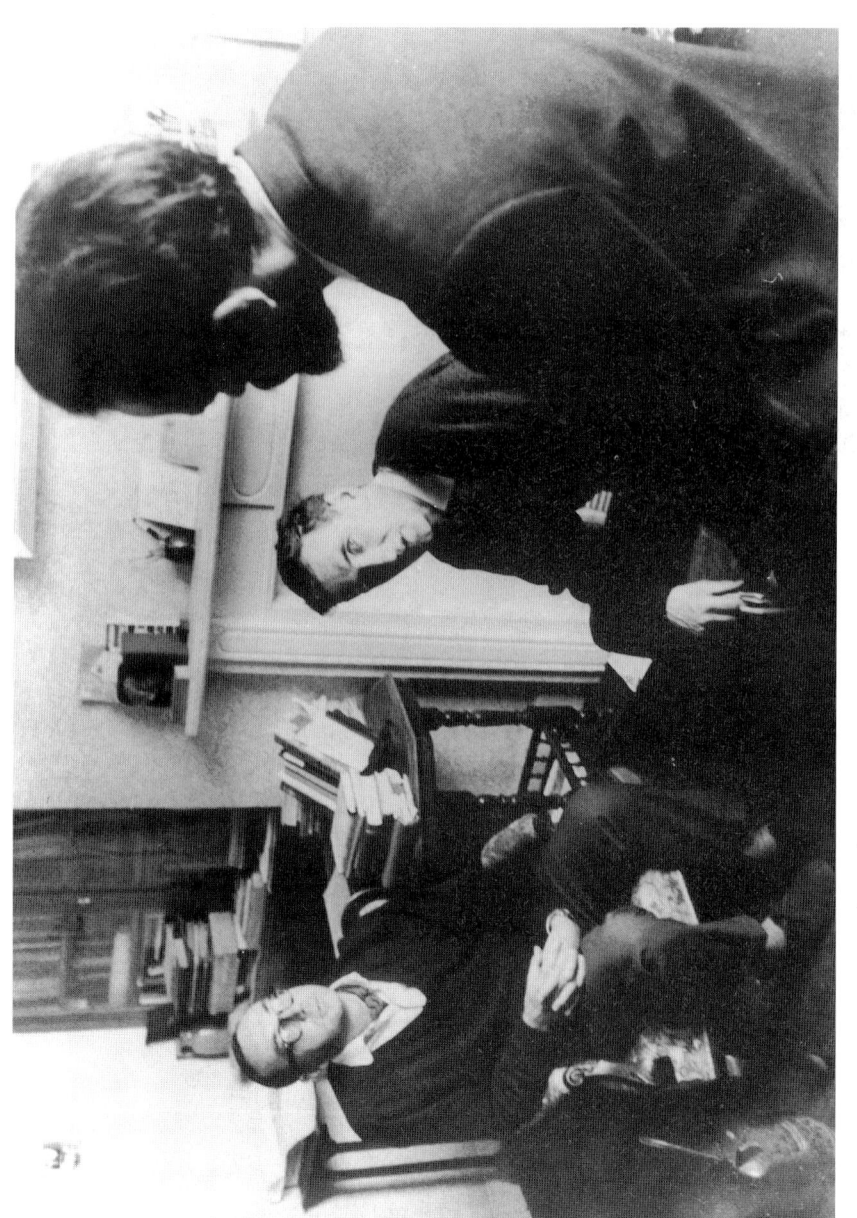

'Like Dolmens...' Tom Kinsella, John Montague, Liam Miller

Brendan, descending

Poet and Diplomat,
Val Iremonger

Norman MacCaig
A Sombre Scot

John Montague and Kafka, 11 Rue Daguerre

Octavio Paz and Kostas, Poet and Philosopher

Tom Kinsella on the Rampart

John Montague, Austin Clarke, Liam Miller on Austin's Seventieth Birthday (9/5/66)

'To John of John Jordan with love, Edward Maguire 23/11/80'

A Lecture from Red Hugh, Peacock Theatre 1970

Heaney, on the Moor

The original poster announcing the first London performance of
The Rough Field

In Full Flight, John Montague and Derek Mahon at the ICA.

Garech Browne and Austin Clarke, Patron and Poet

A Quiet Drink, La Coupole

At the Flore, Poets Claude Esteban and Michel Deguy

The Binder, the Designer and the Pope

John Montague and Queen Victoria!

We were younger, and the booze flowed, but gently, slowed by the music. At the big Fleadh in Boyle, we ate pig's feet from the smeared pages of the *Roscommon Herald*, but then Garech's Indian girlfriend sailed down from Dublin in the Rolls Royce with old-fashioned hampers, which we opened on the nearby Gaelic football pitch, uncovering pots of caviar and bottles of champagne. By now, of course, the Irish wits had christened Garech the Lord of the Fleadhs, and we travelled around with a marvellous retinue of troubadours.

Accommodation was always a problem for our ragged army, and one night we found ourselves in the ultimate godforsaken bog town, where the local publican promised to put us all up on sofas and tables if only Johnny MacDonagh (Sean 'ac Dhonncha from Ahascragh) would sing 'The Bonny Boy'. Our broad, burly host was proud of his nephew, an English television star from *The Prisoner*, and was incensed when the poet Montague confessed complete ignorance of Patrick MacGoohan's existence. To prevent me being flattened by the massive fist of the publican, Johnny had to keep singing 'The Bonny Boy' like a needle stuck on a turntable. The problem of the rough sleeping quarters was complicated by the presence of an already drunk priest, who kept chewing the ears of the younger members of our party, including myself. He ended up with the only double bed going, out of the publican's deep respect for the cloth, and was carried off still mumbling that he would really love some company.

Garech had also developed a passion for carriages, and could be seen cantering though Dublin, perched high upon the coachman's box with his long whip. And there were always parties in the long rooms of his house in the Dublin foothills, Woodtown Manor, which he had taken over from my friend, the American painter

CHAPTER FIVE

Morris Graves. For a whole decade the Claddagh enterprise flourished, and we felt that this splendid balance of hijinks and serious achievement would never falter. It seemed to embody the very spirit of Ireland's version of the 1960s, an old music which had nearly disappeared, gone underground, now flowing through the dignified rooms of an eighteenth-century mansion, with pipers and poets, composers and singers, and whiskey galore in the background. And perhaps a drop of poteen, or moonshine. At my last Fleadh Cheoil, I met the tinker piper Felix Doran, who played a different style, like the Cashes of Wexford, but also, curiously enough, always carried a fiddle. I was on my own, lonely and hungover, when Felix whispered, 'Would you like a drop of the real stuff?' And seeing my puzzlement, he chuckled, 'You know I don't really play the fiddle, but I always carry the case.' Triumphantly he opened it, to display a magnum of vintage poteen. 'A sup will cure your ills.'

When Felix died, all the travelling people from England and Ireland gathered for his funeral: he was their king. British Rail and Irish Shipping had never seen the like, and refused to ferry the revelling mourners home, so they hired a fleet of planes, such was their respect for the old music, and so great their need to see Felix properly down. All over Ireland, the old music had returned, embracing the Yeatsian dream of the Noble and the Beggar Man, and it seemed as if this exuberant, classless party would never end.

> The big house winks over
> the sound, alluring you;
> as does that tiny thatched
> cottage by a rocky lake…

CLADDAGH RAGA

Ways and worlds you
might inhabit, lurching
between sophistication
and innocence, while an

intrigued public lends an ear,
enchanted by such long-
delayed, luxuriantly
sustained ambivalence.

CHAPTER SIX

A CHOSEN LIFE

I
11 Rue Daguerre

In early 1961, Madeleine and I left our small Dublin home. For her own good reasons, Madeleine never really took to Ireland, although she was in at the beginnings of something, a gradual change from the depressed, introverted post-war years to a new energy. But it still seemed meagre compared to the bustle of Paris, and the *mores* of Catholic Ireland struck her as primitive after the sexual sophistication, those natural tributes that men and women paid each other, of her native city. Also there was the Catholic triumphalist *Ne Temere* decree, under which a Catholic and Protestant parent had to swear that they would bring up their children as Catholics, and which Madeleine found appallingly retrograde. (Indeed, while we were still living in Dublin, such rigid triumphalism would erupt in the Fethard-on-Sea boycott of Protestant businesses by their Catholic neighbours.) And her disciplined French mind was dismayed by the exuberant Irish pub life, the dissipation of energies, and the blurring of focus, that inevitably followed a night on the town. I try to analyse her mood in a short story called 'An Occasion of Sin', the last line of which I hesitated over for a long time, since it suggests

CHAPTER SIX

that the protagonist, a young Frenchwoman married to an Irishman, has already decided against returning to his glum city.

I was in two minds (being a Pisces, and therefore prone to indecision) about the move. I had also been impressed by the energy of post-war Paris, had been to hear Juliette Greco sing in the Rose Rouge or the Club Tabou, had glimpsed a bespectacled Sartre working on the terrace of the Flore, and spent over a month in the nearby rue de Rennes. But things were finally warming up in Ireland, so why should I leave? In February 1961, there was a bumper poetry reading in the Hibernian Hotel in Dublin, which illustrates the new mood. Nearly four hundred people packed in to hear Tom Kinsella, Richard Murphy and me, including our two warring senior poets, Clarke and Kavanagh, two government ministers, and a Bishop's wife. Peadar O'Donnell, the Donegal novelist, was our chairman, and he was so pleased that he wanted to induct all three readers into Yeats's Irish Academy of Letters on the spot, and commissioned me to edit a magazine celebrating *la nouvelle vague* of Irish writing.

But I could not easily gainsay Madeleine, especially since she was offering me a new kind of freedom. We had discovered that she could not have children, due to an early operation that was delayed since her father, with his tank regiment at the Front, was not available to give the surgeon permission. Without the expected children to look after, she decided to fold back on her own family and country. And since I did not particularly like working in an office, and she did, she would set me free, provided I completed a PhD, which would give me re-entry into the academy later on, when she wearied.

So I resigned from Bord Failte, and began a study of Goldsmith, as well as a fuller volume of poems for my new editor, Timothy

O'Keefe of MacGibbon and Kee, who also commissioned a book of stories, which would include 'An Occasion of Sin'. Our last year in Herbert Street was hectic, with Goldsmith and the new sheaf of poems alternately spread across the table, and a deluge of visitors, including Robin Skelton, a Yorkshire poet working on Synge manuscripts, and Theodore Roethke from the Pacific Northwest, all clambering down the stairs into our basement.

When it was all cleared and sold off by Madeleine with her usual efficiency, the little flat looked bleak and bereft, an ordinary basement without its African heads, its rush matting and anglepoise lamps, which had given it a charming French look. Our new found friend Garech Browne, who had taken to dropping in at all hours of the day and night, with the strangest of friends with the strangest of names, like 'The Shit Mackey' and 'Horrible Joe', declared that it was the most desolate sight he had ever seen. Our beloved tomcat was dispatched to the French Ambassador's Residence, where at least he would be well fed. (We learnt later that he was killed by a car while in pursuit of the Ambassador's poodle.)

*

We stayed with Madeleine's mother for over a month, within sight, of course, of the *Ecole Militaire* and the *Champ de Mars*, since they were a military family, and where I brought their pure-bred spaniel for a walk twice a day. I was a bit homesick, so I chatted to their maid, a little girl from County Carlow, whom we had found for *la Comtesse*, Madeleine's tall and equine mother. And daily we searched for a new home, which we finally found in a courtyard in the rue Daguerre, an atelier occupied by a splendid Greek philosopher called Kostas Papaiannou, who seemed to know everything

CHAPTER SIX

and everyone under the sun. They were moving out because their child found the steep, galley-like studio stairs too difficult. We could not move in, however, for another month, so they placed us in their new unfinished apartment, which unfortunately was close to a major intersection, with the traffic churning through my uneasy sleep.

I was trying to put down roots again, deciphering Ponge and Guillevic in neighbourhood cafés, and negotiating to do a 'Letter from Paris' for the *Irish Times*. We called on the American architect of the building and his wife in their penthouse apartment. They also were childless, and she had taken to breeding birds, which balanced on her wrist, leather jesses laced over her white arm, as she sipped her gin. It was in this grey part of Paris that we all waited for news of the putsch of the Algerian generals. There were soldiers in the streets, tanks in the Concorde, and I glimpsed Malraux's pale face at a ministerial window.

*

At last we moved into the cloistered privacy of the rue Daguerre, away from Madeleine's imperious mother and the din of traffic. The rue Daguerre was one of the best open market streets in Paris, bright with canopied stalls during the morning, bustling with fervid shoppers clutching rush baskets, enjoying to the full the banter of the fishmonger or the cheese merchant extolling their wares. The contrast between that crowded clamorous market and our little courtyard was magical.

An unobtrusive green door opened in the wall beside the florists. As it clanged behind you, you found yourself in a leafy enclave, a series of low studios of which ours was the last, with glass panels in the ceilings through which light could pour, ideal for artists, and writers like myself. The wire netting of a bird sanctuary enclosed a tree, in which minute budgerigars chirped and exchanged seed like love tokens. (When I looked up their name in the dictionary, I was pleased to learn that it is the aborigine word for 'bird of love'.) A series of small stone heads, left by an absconding sculptor as part payment for his lodgings, paraded along the length of the courtyard. And outside our door was a cherry tree, which would flower in the spring:

> In that stillness – soft but luminously exact,
> A chosen light – I notice that
> The tips of the lately grafted cherry tree
>
> Are a firm and lacquered black.

Slowly, I settled in. Writers take a while to transplant, and I had left most of my books behind me in Ireland, but I had already contracted to write the book of stories that would become *Death of a Chieftain*. And there were the beginnings of a long poem, which would take me a decade to finish. In a way, my bluff had been called: I had always wanted to be a writer, and here I was with nothing else to do except write, in this idyllic framework. And the studio had been the workplace of Kostas before me, so the walls were used to brooding. In the morning, Madeleine would leave for her office after our twin bowls of *café au lait* and croissants or *tartines*. Then I had the whole morning to myself, to read and write to my heart's content while a light rain pattered on the glass roof, with no distractions unless our new Siamese cat, Kafka, decided he needed caresses or conversation where he curled beside me on a stool.

CHAPTER SIX

*

Weekends we went to stay with Madeleine's seemingly endless family, immured in the Normandy countryside. It was astonishing for someone like myself, from a family broken by Northern Irish politics, to observe the ramifications of the d'Avoust clan. The old Duke, still spry in his eighties, dwelt in their nondescript chateau, Bellozanne, with whatever members of his large family seemed to be around, from Leopold ('Dop' for short), the eldest son, to Guy and Christiane, the youngest, who were roughly my own age. Counting husbands, wives and children, the inhabitants amounted to a small army, encamped on a terrain with which it had little contact anymore, although, when younger, the Duke had been mayor of the local village.

Madeleine's mother, Marguerite, was the Duke's eldest child, but, being female, could not succeed; she lived with her husband, a retired colonel, in a large dower house near the family chapel where Madeleine and I had been married. She had created a large family as well, six children including Madeleine, and they were also acquiring wives or husbands and children: to keep up with it all, to memorise the names and titles of all the in-laws, was like being in some old-fashioned history lesson. I was surprised to find myself in the French stud book, *Le Bottin Mondaine*, as *Monsieur John Montague*, next to my wife's more formidable entry.

I did my best to read the social register right, and they were welcoming enough to me, because they had a soft spot for Ireland. There had been a long tradition of Irish nurses in the family whom they had preferred to English nannies because they were Catholic. Indeed, when Madeleine's mother had come to Dublin, to visit us in Herbert Street and stay in that small back room, we had brought her to see an old family retainer on the North Side, in Austin Clarke's Mountjoy Street. It was a strange sight, the big-boned, handsome French lady bending down over the gnarled little old Dublin woman who had looked after her as a baby. Indeed, she had taught the d'Avoust children prayers in Irish, which emerged now as a kind of mnenomic gibberish, a family joke at the table or in the salon. It took me a long time to work out, for example, that what they called 'packet of nish' was *peacaid anios*, from the 'Our Father' in Irish.

The day in Bellozanne was structured around the two major meals, with usually eight or nine *à table*, depending on the visitors: *Monsieur le Curé*, after Sunday Mass, hoisting his black skirts over the stove; the Duke if he decided to visit his eldest daughter, whose table was usually better than in the family chateau. After breakfast, the morning was spent in the dairy town of Gournay-en-Bray, where Madeleine and her mother conducted the time-honoured French ritual of shopping for meals in the open-air markets. After lunch, everyone moved to the salon, which was followed by a siesta before the preparations for the evening meal began.

On good days we walked through the woods with their many alleys named like streets after historical events or other members of the extended family, which included the descendants of the other Napoleonic marshals, since, scorned by the pre-revolutionary nobility, they tended to marry amongst themselves, *les boulevards extérieurs*. The main subject for discussion was always the family, analysed endlessly in every detail, in a manner that now seems to me typically French. Weddings or funerals were particularly impressive, with the whole front of the church taken over by throngs of relatives, a great exfoliating tree, to which my own bough had been recently grafted.

Between these two poles, the secret courtyard of *onze, rue Daguerre*, and the d'Avoust seat in Normandy, I lived out my French life, city and country, bohemian and bourgeois. My second volume of poems, *Poisoned Lands*, came out in London in 1961, and the Counsellor, Val Iremonger, threw a splendid party at the Irish Embassy in Grosvenor Square, where I met some of my London contemporaries, like Anthony Burgess, Anthony Hartley, Robert Conquest and a saturnine Louis MacNeice, who would become a friend, though too briefly, alas, due to his early death. Iremonger, a poet himself, was a great help, including a story of mine, 'That Dark Accomplice', to end his new edition of *The Faber Book of Short Stories*.

(There is a story behind that story. As a younger writer in Dublin, I had hovered between poetry, my first love, but a prospect the economic implications of which frightened me, and prose, which at least offered the possibility of some readership, and some money. After all, most of my elders were professional storytellers, O'Flaherty, O'Faolain, O'Connor, and now my only literary friend from Tyrone, Ben Kiely. *Dubliners* especially fascinated me, and I wondered if I could write as exactly and truthfully as that, so I began to bang out stories on my black Royal typewriter. Stories about sex, of course, which I did not dare show round at that time, in that place. We might pass around copies of *Tropic of Cancer*, or other supposedly 'dirty' books, as long as they were foreign. But we were overly cautious about showing our own more daring work, because of the harsh prudery prevailing in our little post-Colonial society. For instance, a harmless novel by Benedict Kiely, *In a Harbour Green*, had already been banned by the Censorship Board, as being 'in its general tendency, indecent or obscene'. But one story about my schooldays in Armagh began to flow, as if by magic, and I brought the first half into Peadar O'Donnell, then editor of *The Bell*. Peadar approved, and said that he would pay me fifteen pounds when it was finished, three weeks' salary for me in those dim days. Elated, I tore on, and bore it in to him triumphantly. Alas, he said that he could not credit the main character, a sadistic priest! No publication and no pence: I took a vow that I would never publish another story until 'That Dark Accomplice' appeared. A vow from which Iremonger released me after ten years, with his *Faber* anthology, thus enabling me to resume the collection of stories that would become *Death of a Chieftain*, for Tim O'Keefe.)

*

Settling in, I was getting to know my rue Daguerre neighbours. There was a veteran of the First World War, Auguste Carrier, who lived with his buxom wife in a much smaller studio, and painted genteel, old-fashioned studies of landscapes and nudes, including an idealised, rosy portrait of Mme Carrier. He did not sell at all except to a dwindling number of relatives, and newer acquaintances like us. We bought one to hang discreetly above the hall stand, where he would be pleased to see it when he called in for one of his ritual recountings of woes.

The *artiste-peintre* in the studio next door *did* sell, but in the tourist stalls of Montmartre: a genial Italian, he had a picture postcard nailed to his easel, which he faithfully reproduced every two days for gullible foreigners delighted by these original depictions of *le vraie France*. He wore a paint-stained smock, and, when he left with his masterpieces under his arm, sported a drooping red

CHAPTER SIX

beret. Auguste complained bitterly about him and about Bellegarde, a quite well-known younger painter who also had a studio in our courtyard. I took tea with Bellegarde occasionally, and discussed Mallarmé, for whom he had a profound devotion; the blank space of the page and the canvas being equally threatening. He painted medium-sized abstracts, often pure white with stains and splotches of colour, like blood on a starched shirtfront; honourable work in a late modern style, which made M. Carrier weep with thwarted rage, deflected only by mention of the Italian's latest imitative *chef d'oeuvre*, which would compel him to clutch his brow.

Pauvre Auguste: slight and handsome and totally out of date, he more than anyone I have ever known deserved the *sobriquet* 'Knight of the Dolorous Countenance'. As the decade came to its turbulent close, we would help to send Auguste and his missus, encumbered with all his old-fashioned painting paraphernalia, easel, tubes of paint and brushes, on their annual holiday to some remote part of France where he might find what he called a 'motif' before the bulldozers rolled in. But usually it was too late, and we would receive long, plaintive missives about how speed and noise had ravaged even the most obscure countryside in the Lot or the Cantal.

But our most profound friendship was with Denise and Claude Esteban, who lived directly across the way from us. Denise was from Rheims, a cathedral city I knew from my hostelling days; myself and a Derry lad had gone there to celebrate after working on the Marne champagne harvest, before descending on our bicycles into Paris. She was charming, not conventionally beautiful, but vivacious, with a throaty, sensuous laugh. She taught art, and had begun to paint herself, but with great diffidence. Denise was very popular, and the clang of her door, as suitors came and went, was a feature of our early days in the rue Daguerre. But soon the clang stopped, when she married Claude Esteban, a gifted young poet of Basque origin, who taught Spanish literature at the Sorbonne, yet wrote in French. Dark-eyed, eloquent, garlanded in the ubiquitous French intellectual's scarf, Claude was nearly as learned as Kostas. Over the years, our friendship would deepen, as we shared holidays in the Vaucluse, near Sade's Lacoste, or they came to Ireland, where Denise first began to paint in earnest.

Esteban was the first to introduce me to the contemporary poetic life of Paris. He was a friend and admirer of Yves Bonnefoy, who sometimes came to lunch across the way. Claude was ebullient, enthusiastic, a contrast to the grave, hermetical Bonnefoy. Yves, nonetheless, paid careful attention to the translations Claude and Madeleine were making of my poems for the N.R.F., and it was exciting to see an early chestnut like 'The Water Carrier' in its new guise as *'Le Porteur d'Eau'*. Or Claude's magnificent translation, *'Dolmens, autour de mon Enfance, Vieilles Gens'*, with its procession of ancient Ulster eccentrics tottering through the pages of the most illustrious French literary journal, the magazine of Gide and Proust. I was trying to promote my contemporaries, as well, to give a glimpse of the new literary energy in Ireland, so that when another series of Montague translations appeared in *Preuves*, the French equivalent of *Encounter*, the review also included Claude's translations of Austin Clarke and Thomas Kinsella. Introducing the latter, Claude delivered an extraordinary judgement, describing Tom as *'un beau tempérament poétique ... chevalier servant d'un solipsisme implacable.'* In return, I translated some of Claude's fine, gloomy poems from *La Saison Dévastée* (a title almost as cheerful as my own *Poisoned Lands*).

French literary life seemed to be very ritualised, with afternoon receptions at the various leading journals, very much like the

CHAPTER SIX

literary evenings of Yeats's Dublin, or like the 'At Homes' and calling cards of Proust's Paris. Or so it struck me, at a distance, since my French was not then equal to such formal occasions. Unlike my neighbour, Samuel Beckett, I had not studied French, since it was not yet part of the curriculum of St Patrick's, Armagh. So my French was increasingly fluent, but not grammatical, learnt mainly through conversations with friends, especially Madeleine. And of course most of my friends and acquaintances had school English, which they were amused to practise on me. ('*Dîtes* "yes",' Madeleine's old family *curé* had encouraged, when I stammered over the '*Oui*' in our marriage ceremony. '*C'est la même chose.*')

But then the whole issue of the colloquial and the formal in French was a vexing problem. What impressed me about Beckett's trilogy was that he wrote the kind of informal French that I used to hear spoken at the *zinc* of *La Chope Daguerre*, the most casual bar in our neighbourhood. And I gathered that it had taken the experience of the War to shake him free of the restrictions of his academic French, whereas most of the French writers I met seemed to feel that one had to enter into a special state of mind, above and beyond the ordinary, before committing oneself to the page: *L'Ecriture*. Again and again, Beckett would recommend Céline to me for his directness, hardly a writer you would have expected Sam to approve of, since Céline was known to be anti-Semitic and a fascist, but he loved his supple, casual prose.

The same strictures seemed to operate for English: again and again I met French professors of English who spoke as if Queen Victoria were still alive, carrying the exactness and formality of their own training into that more flexible and inclusive language. I had a personal interest in this problem, and not only because of my own faltering efforts to speak, and sometimes write, in the language of the country I was now living in. I was coaching Madeleine, after her Honours MA English thesis in Iowa, on the American war novel, for that strange French exam, *l'Agrégation*, which was crucial to anyone aspiring to a university career in France. By now she was fluent in American, Irish and British English; if she could keep up with Behan or Louis MacNeice, I thought, she was ready for any French interrogation. But the better English she read and spoke, the less well she did in that absurd exam, and again and again I came up against the mystique and, to me, tyranny, of *les Grandes Ecoles*, in French society. Simone de Beauvoir's near subservience to Sartre seemed to me to be based on his having beaten her to first place in the *Agrégation*, although she was several years younger, and it was his second try, having been defeated by Aron in the first – and of course he had to quarrel with Aron. I had never known a society like this, where one's performance in a single exam determined the course of a whole career, intellectual, literary, even emotional.

It recalled my own old rivalries at University College, Dublin, with John Jordan and Denis Donoghue in English, and F.X. Martin in History, which have echoed down the years, though with much less determined bitterness. Perhaps biographers and scholars should look to the school room for the origins of literary disputes in later years? For we are cast as in a constellation with our contemporaries, whose passage across the skies encourages or disturbs us, with the whole pattern only gradually becoming clear.

II
Beyond the Courtyard

The Algerian conflict dominated our early years in Paris, always smouldering in the background. Once, when Madeleine woke up in

CHAPTER SIX

Dublin to the sound of an explosion, crying 'What's that?', I soothed her by explaining that it was just another statue being blown up, peremptorily expunged in a new IRA campaign against any vestige of British rule in Ireland. So poor Nelson, whom nearly everybody by now had adopted as an honorary Dubliner, was toppled from the top of his pillar, and the magnificent equestrian statue of Field Marshal Gough, at the entrance to the Phoenix Park, was blown to smithereens, when it could have been simply renamed 'Irishman on Horse'.

Madeleine had taken it as more of the antics of the wild Irish, but here we now were in the heart of Paris, coming awake to a not-so-distant thud and the hee-haw of sirens, as another building was *plastiqué*, the new style of home-made bombing which would soon become universal.

Thanks to the lofty brilliance of de Gaulle, the *pieds noirs* (the Orangemen of Algeria) were being outmanoeuvred, although their sullen defiance would still sound through the streets of France, as they blared their klaxons to the beat of 'O.A.S.' (*l'Organisation de l'armée secrète*), or 'Al-gé-rie-fran-çaise'. The intransigence of the FLN was paying off, but the struggle on their side was not easy either. On the other, or 'wrong' half of our street, there were many North Africans, and I often lunched in their cafés, watching the belly dancers gyrate on the juke box, or listening to their wailing songs (which Sean Ó Riada loved so much), as the exiles ate their highly spiced, aromatic meals. Sometimes there were tensions between blue-eyed Kabylien moderates from the Mountains of the Moon, and the more determined FLN, country against city, or so it seemed to an outsider like myself. One of my favourite Arab restaurants was raked with machine gun fire, Chicago style, so I felt that I should bring my patronage elsewhere, since I could not distinguish between the MNA and the FLN in their transplanted civil war.

As an Ulsterman, I could appreciate some of their problems, and still regret that I did not persuade the *Irish Times* to send me to Algeria. Even in Madeleine's military family, there was an unease about how the war was being waged, with the army using torture to combat street terrorism, a glimpse of French 'valour' at variance with the legend of the graduates of St Cyr riding out gallantly, in their white gloves, to face the tanks. And Madeleine did not want me going to the more violent street demonstrations, like the 17th October 1961, at the Pont de Neuilly, or the 19th December at the place de la Bastille. It was a tense period, the riot police lining the streets, the CRS with their long batons like billy clubs, as the unarmed protesters approached. There were rumours – which turned out to be true – of bodies thrown in the Seine, after a police massacre near the metro Charonne, with its echoes of Charon, boatman across the Styx, and *charogne*, French for carrion. For reasons I could not fathom, it was obvious that the French were not at ease with their North African Arab neighbours, *les sales bicots* being considered far inferior to *les nègres*. It had to do with France's complicated colonial past, the African-French regiments, who, according to one of Madeleine's uncles, 'fought very well when trained', and a familial sympathy for France's largely conscript army, struggling against a guerrilla force in a war even nastier than Indo-China. Certainly, from my own background, I could understand that religion and race are an incendiary mix.

What a contrast with the lofty press conferences of President Charles de Gaulle, which I was now entitled to attend as an accredited Correspondent: I believe I was the only Irish journalist there. De Gaulle fascinated me, as someone capable of manipulating

CHAPTER SIX

his own legend, speaking sonorously of 'La France', as an old-fashioned romantic poet might summon his Muse. Like De Valera, he believed that he incarnated the spirit of his country, but de Gaulle seemed to me to have the saving grace of an extraordinary sense of humour, partly mocking himself with his grandiloquent gesticulations and Gallic groans and shrugs. He was even taller than De Valera, and certainly more portly, a man who loved the table. (According to Madeleine, meals at the Elysée were reputed to be excellent, but de Gaulle insisted that they should be eaten expeditiously, no more than thirty minutes for lunch.) He used his height to dominate his distinguished ministers, even the twitching visage of that other legend, André Malraux, who seemed almost small beside his master. It was great theatre, clearly all well thought out and planned in advance, with planted questions. I tried to introduce my penny-worth at some point, only to be batted aside like a fly, although once he nodded in my direction, 'M. le Temps Irlandais.'

De Gaulle seemed to me a Great Comedian, to borrow Yeats's phrase, and in my mind he was always shadowed by the equally tall, antediluvian figure of Jacques Tati, whose comically lugubrious, hound-dog face was uncannily similar to that of the great leader. Old-fashioned, almost a dinosaur, Tati was everyone's favourite mad uncle, mocking the illusion of progress, and determined to catch up with the Americans on his postman's bicycle, an ambition also preached by Charles de Gaulle with his independent *'force de frappe'*. Madeleine's military family did not entirely approve of Charles of the Gauls; as regular army, they resented what they saw as his self-promotion from colonel to general. Whereas I thought he showed the visionary genius of a poet in his early writings about the future of mechanised warfare, which, unfortunately, were read and applied only by the German High Command.

It was a heady business for a country lad from County Tyrone, to be living in such a great society with so many layers and levels. Madeleine now worked at the *Patronat*, the union of French employers, and we were invited to many formal meals, where I learnt how to fillet a fish, and eat a peach with knife and fork. (Madeleine's father, asked his opinion of his prospective son-in-law, had only commented that he had observed me *'saloper un poisson'*, or 'fuck up a fish', which apparently was a judgement on my character, country and upbringing.) French table etiquette was even more mysterious and elaborate than the English, and I learnt the rules mechanically, the way a horse learns to clear hurdles.

The conversation was as highly structured and formal as the meals, general at the start, with much comment on the makes and speeds of new French cars; then a discreet discussion of the arts towards the end of the main course, so as not to interfere with the digestion. Violent and disruptive subjects, like the latest writings of Jean-Paul or Simone on the Algerian problem, were rarely raised, just as there was little analysis of the French collapse during the Second World War, or their abandonment of the Jews at Drancy. We stayed mainly on safe ground, but that safe ground could sometimes be marvellous, as when we attended a Hunting Mass at the country home of Jean-Jacques Guerlain, the hunting horns sounding through the church.

Madeleine was very popular, and moved through her society with ease, managing to bring me with her as exotic baggage, an Irish poet indeed. *'Elle se paye le luxe d'avoir un poète comme mari'*: she could afford the luxury of having a poet husband, said a senior official in her office. And I blundered, betimes, unused to the richness of the social diet. Madeleine loved to swim, for example, and at lunchtime during the summer we would often meet at the fashionable

CHAPTER SIX

swimming pool in the Seine, *les Bains Deligny*, where bronzed bodies briefly plunged before arranging themselves to sunbathe on beach towels. We got to know an official from the Russian Embassy, who liked to speak English with us, but I drove him off by asking gauchely, 'What exactly do you do at the Embassy?'

Another high point was when we were asked to the annual garden party at the British Embassy, a very handsome building with extensive grounds. Suddenly I spied a frail, rather forlorn-looking little man, a bit like a pet dog that had seen better days: it was Eddie Windsor, the exiled Prince of Wales. I have to confess that I felt a *frisson*, shaking hands with someone who had been, albeit in a negative way, involved in the unmaking of English history. The drama of his abdication had been part of my Ulster boyhood; after all, despite my Catholic nationalist background, I had also been a little British boy, listening to the BBC as well as Radio Eireann. We were joined by a group of journalists, of course, one from the *Daily Express*, and again I spoiled matters by announcing cheerfully that I had taken a successful libel action against them. As far as everyone was concerned, including Madeleine, this was a serious conversation stopper, in an atmosphere dedicated to the tinkling of teacups and trivial exchanges. Clearly I had put my *pieds dans le plat*.

Art openings were also very formal, with little or no alcohol served, astonishing to someone used to Dublin or London openings, where abundant wine was the first criterion for a successful launch. The most illustrious was the Galerie Maeght, rue Teheran, where, for a major *vernissage*, like Francis Bacon, the room would be crowded with some of the most distinguished and gifted artists and critics in the world, beginning with Francis himself. Brassai I already vaguely knew, because he lived around the corner, and Cartier-Bresson I had helped to guide through Dublin in my Bord Failte days. (I had brought him to photograph the shark tank of McDaid's, which interested him so much he balanced on his toes to get a better shot. As a contrast, I had also brought him to a meeting of the mighty editorial committee of the Dolmen Miscellany: myself, Tom Kinsella and Liam Miller.) William Hayter, the engraver, was there with Désirée, and the le Brocquys if they were in town from their home above Nice.

And Bonnefoy and Esteban in their capacity as art critics, an occupation highly esteemed in France. French poets in general seemed to be deeply involved in the world of visual arts, the director of the gallery being another distinguished younger poet, Jacques Dupin. An occasional glass of champagne might appear, but the atmosphere was intensely serious, and the artist involved would be honoured with a magnificent illustrated tribute. It was in this way I came to meet the work of artists like Ubac and Chilida, as yet unknown in Ireland.

One evening, the Hayters and I brought along Patrick Collins, an Irish painter on his uppers in Paris, to a Maeght opening. All the big guns were there, including Miro, and they seemed so pleased to see one another that they adjourned to a friendly café. Paddy became very silent, and embarrassed us by producing a little sketchbook, where he began to make rough pencil portraits of his companions, like a street artist. The artists concerned were a bit disconcerted, but, being French-trained, they were too polite to comment. We questioned him afterwards as discreetly as we could, where he thought he was, and what he was doing. Humbly, Paddy replied, 'I found myself among the gods, and I felt I had to make a note of it.'

There were also the big exhibitions. During his stay at the Mexican Embassy in Paris, the poet Octavio Paz launched an extraordinary survey of Mexican art in the Grand Palais. Paz was

CHAPTER SIX

also a friend of Kostas, and the exhibition brought back for Madeleine and myself our long summer in Mexico. He would resign from the diplomatic service over the Olympics scandal, when the students were massacred, but his stay in Paris seemed to be happy and eventful. Paz was also translated into French by Esteban, and in our house in Ballydehob I still have a shadowy, scarlet surrealist painting by his wife Bona, who had previously been married to André-Pieyre de Mandiargues, poet and writer. Paz had also written a poem on our rue Daguerre studio, in memory of his evenings there with Kostas.

It was a rich scene, but the greatest concentration of talent, I gradually and gratefully began to recognise, was in our own part of Paris. Sartre had moved down from Saint-Germain to avoid the bombs, and Simone was close by, in the rue Schoelcher. (Algren had said that we should look her up, but Madeleine was busy and my French still faltering.) And Beckett, I had begun to realise, lived around the corner, in the Boulevard St Jacques. Walking past the American bar of the Dome one day, I saw him and Giacometti, their two austere heads tilted towards each other. And Ionesco and his Asian wife would come wandering by on the Boulevard Raspail; he had a weakness for Ireland, and would come to Saint Patrick's Day parties at the Embassy, a strange scene, I found, where all the old Irish nannies in Paris would assemble and get paralytic on whiskey in their Going-to-Mass grandeur, button boots and all.

Through this society I swam, a relatively unknown fish, flexing its fins in these larger waters. A thriving artistic community should be normal, the example of your peers provoking you to greater efforts, but I was not used to the effortless tact and discretion. I *was* used to the idea of an artistic *quartier*, but, while Kavanagh and Behan might have been neighbours, they were often not speaking to each other, and Flann O'Brien (Brian O'Nolan) could rear like a serpent. Now I was happily busy, the best state for a writer, assembling *The Dolmen Miscellany* (1961), the first of my anthologies. It would contain the opening chapters of the two first novels of the two most promising novelists of our generation, John MacGahern and Aidan Higgins, and two longer poems by my poetic contemporaries, Richard Murphy and Tom Kinsella, with a critical essay by myself on Goldsmith to set a standard. The short stories were coming, and were beginning to be published in the literary magazines of Paris, like Les Lettres Nouvelles. One story they printed, 'The Cry' (*Le Cri*), was probably the first about police violence in the North of Ireland. In writing it, I had been influenced not only by my own beleaguered North, but also my experience of the tense Paris of that time.

So I was slowly establishing a fertile dialogue between my old and new worlds, Ireland and France. My English editor, Timothy O'Keefe, helped, seeking my advice about the revival of Irish writers who had fallen out of favour and print, partly because of the War, like Flann O'Brien. He also asked me to read a lengthy memoir by Francis Stuart. While I found it fascinating, something about the first-person voice troubled me, since it seemed to lack a necessary narrative distance, was too close to the bone. I rejected it reluctantly, but, sure enough, it appeared some years later as that ambiguous classic, *Black List, Section H*, transposed, successfully I thought, to a third-person voice. This more aloof narrator, presenting us with a main character who is something of a Holy Fool, was a much better approach than the previous version, in which there seemed to be no perspective on the troubling anti-hero.

Another of Tim O'Keefe's requests gave me serious pause: he wanted me to help edit the collected poems of Patrick Kavanagh from behind the scenes, a task which was bound to have reverberations. And the shadowy shape of my long poem beckoned me on, to muster all my technical energies in order to express an emerging historical and personal vision.

Yes, we seemed happy, and, one day, Kostas and his wife came by to pay homage to their old haunt.

'When we were here,' they told Madeleine, '*On petait de bonheur*,' or, 'We farted with joy.'

Indeed, perhaps we understood the sentiment behind their Rabelaisian salvo of praise for our sheltered courtyard. So why then would I ever leave it, especially with the friendly presence of our greatest writer just around the corner?

CHAPTER SEVEN

SAMUEL BECKETT, NEIGHBOUR

Off Stage

Hugh Kenner has a book on T.S. Eliot, the invisible poet. For us, growing up in the 1940s and early 1950s in Ireland, Samuel Beckett was the Invisible Writer, the Greta Garbo of modern literature. None of his work was in print. There was a grim story going the rounds that he had been stabbed in Paris, and a party given in the Bailey by Oliver St John Gogarty to celebrate his possible demise. Austin Clarke told me that he had nearly taken a libel action against Beckett's English publisher because of the cruel portrait of him as Austin Ticklepenny, the Pot Poet of Dublin, in the novel *Murphy*, and Austin still referred to him as Sam Bucket. Then, at a Dublin party, I met Con Leventhal and his wife, Eithna McCarthy, both of whom I already knew of as contributers to the *Dublin Magazine*, where some of my own early poems had appeared. They both spoke warmly of their great friend and contemporary at Trinity, and encouraged me to look him up in Paris in an obscure street, something like 'Favourite'? For I was planning my attack on post-war France, with a rucksack and a new racing bicycle I had bought with the proceeds of an English literature prize.

Although banned in Ireland, copies of *Murphy* were being passed from hand to hand. I found one myself in the stalls of Charing Cross, only to have it snaffled by a brother poet, the same who later kept my first edition of *Under the Volcano*, so he had good taste. I also found a copy of Beckett's youthful essay on Proust, a lovely little book with a dolphin on the cover. But my real triumph was to arrange to have myself locked in the back room of the National Library, where all the banned books were racked like slumbering bombs. 'The fiercest literary censorship this side of the Iron Curtain – and I do not exclude Spain,' wrote Robert Graves from Majorca in a letter to the *Irish Times* in 1950.

I would take this strange scene as a symbol of the intellectual isolation of our new neo-Catholic state, which had helped to drive Beckett out of Ireland. In search of a prose *persona*, I hovered between the scholastic arrogance of Stephen Dedalus and Belacqua, the prone polyglot protagonist of *More Pricks Than Kicks*. I have since re-found the cryptic epigrams I culled during that curious isolation, like 'Any fool can turn the blind eye, but who knows what the ostrich sees in the sand?' and they can still turn my head.

When I first began to explore France, in 1948, and later, in 1950 during the so-called Holy Year, I enquired about Beckett, but there was little to learn. Con Leventhal said that Beckett had brought a new novel out of the war, but I could not track him down, as I did Francis and Madeleine Stuart, in their *chambre de bonne*, near the *Ecole Militaire*. I read Francis a self-absorbed new poem of my own on suffering and starvation – 'In learning hunger one learns other things' – while their Siamese cats mated noisily in the background. But extracts from *Watt* were appearing in the little magazines of the post-war period, like John Ryan's *Envoy* in Dublin, and *Merlin* in Paris. There was a small group around that review: Patrick Bowles (who later was to help to translate *Molloy* into English), Austryn Wainhouse, Richard Seaver, a lean Scot called Alex Trocchi, all of whom spoke of Beckett, and some of whom had glimpsed, or even met him, with his polo neck and prison haircut. And of course Sinbad Vail, the son of Peggy Guggenheim, had also heard of him, although Beckett did not appear in his little yellow-covered review, *Points*, where early Behan erotica had been published. I did find two copies of Georges Duthuit's post-war *Transition* with his extraordinary *Three Dialogues* on art with Beckett, where the Frenchman serves as a stooge for Beckett's uncompromising views, startling to a starter like myself, but echoing some of the more intransigent theorems in his Proust essay. (One of the copies contains a bleak prose monologue by Suzanne Dumesnil, Beckett's future wife, which sounds like his later self; clearly they thought alike.)

As my Dublin pals poured into Saint-Germain that summer of 1950, they met, and occasionally mated, with the French lot, and the new wave of American ex-pats. Daniel Mauroc, the poet of the *quartier*, strode by in his black cloak. We heard about Richard Wright, we saw James Baldwin, but there was nary a sign of Beckett, and of course I had lost his address. Already the myth of the aloof hermit was growing, and there was a rumour that he was writing in French, having given up English in disgust. I would not be around when the shock of *Godot* began to reverberate in the salons: I had fled as far away as San Francisco.

In the Wings

Little did I know that, a decade later, this mysterious recluse would be my neighbour: I define 'neighbour' as someone living nearby or nigh. After the move to our rue Daguerre studio in 1961, I began to recognise my artistic neighbours. There was Eugene Guillevic, the poet from Brittany, plump as a bullfrog but walking with delicate steps; lean Bill Hayter, the engraver, an old Cornish hand; Brassai, writer, artist, photographer of the old night life and walls of Paris; smiling Ionesco with his Asian wife; Simone de Beauvoir in her sober garb, like a lay sister. Such a concentration of genius in a small area was characteristic of Montparnasse; Picasso, Mondrian, Grosz and Chirico had all lived in the *quartier* a few decades before.

It was against this background that I finally glimpsed Beckett. Passing the American bar of the Dome, I came to a halt as I saw two heads bent together in close colloquy, Beckett and Giacometti, who also lived nearby, with his brother Diego. I knew they liked each other, but to see them huddled together so intently was awesome, Beckett's stripped profile and Alberto's corrugated countenance. Were they discussing the tree in the Odéon production of *Godot*, or the racing results of the PMU?

I also became conscious that Beckett, like myself, was a great walker. I would see him here or there walking through the city, often far from our home base. One day I glimpsed him by the children's pool in the Luxembourg Gardens, standing still as a heron, watching the toy boats. The conventions of our village, our *quartier*, which I was beginning to understand, demanded discretion, so I passed by, but was moved enough to write a sonnet, 'Salute in Passing', which is almost transparent in meaning compared with Beckett's own more oblique and learned poems.

> The voyagers we cannot follow
> Are the most haunting. That face
> Time has worn to a fastidious mask
> Chides me, as one strict master
> Steps through the Luxembourg.
> Surrounded by children, lovers,
> His thoughts are rigorous as trees

> Reduced by winter. While the water
> Parts for tiny white-rigged yachts
> He plots an icy human mathematics –
> Proving what content sighs when all
> Is lost, what wit flares from nothingness:
> His handsome Aztec head is sacrificial
> As he weathers to how man is.

At that time I was editing that anthology of the *nouvelle vague* of Irish writing, and I dropped off the bold, red-covered *Dolmen Miscellany* at 38, Boulevard Saint Jacques, just round the corner, and a correspondence began. Beckett's epistolary style was to the point. He liked the anthology, approved of its aims, and my own essay on Goldsmith had given him 'great pleasure'. Heady stuff for a younger writer to hear, so I took my heart in my hands and sent him the Luxembourg Gardens poem. He liked that too, and soon we were arranging to meet, now and again, on neutral ground for a chat. Everything connected with those early meetings was punctilious and formal. I called him between twelve and one, and he suggested a meeting place, usually nearby, the Closerie des Lilas, a well-appointed temple to literature with its commemorative plaques everywhere, or the side bar of La Coupole.

I remember very little of what we said, except our seemingly mutual embarrassment. Mr Beckett was painfully shy, shy as an adolescent, twitching, touching things, rearranging objects on the table, a nervous habit of my own, so that it began to look like a game of phantom chess. In his essay on Proust, which had just been reprinted, and which I had reviewed in *The Guardian*, he seemed to argue that conversation was impossible, with an always changing subject confronting an eternally shifting object. And since I was not involved in the theatre, I had little or no Green Room gossip. Besides, I stammered, so we found ourselves in the absurd situation of someone who found it hard to speak engaging someone who did not believe in conversation, and certainly not in small talk. Sometimes there were long silences between us, as though we were gazing together down some deep well.

But though I felt vaguely uneasy about these silences, we gradually found common ground. We discussed Synge, whom he described as 'a nice man', like Goldsmith; he was especially fond of his prose writings on Wicklow, and spoke warmly of some of the lesser-known plays, like *The Well of the Saints*. I began to realise that Beckett's late and unexpected success as a dramatist was based on his student years in Dublin. He described how he would slip away to attend first nights in the Abbey, including several of the Yeats plays, and the controversial early performance of *The Plough and the Stars* in 1926, when he was only nineteen. The old Abbey seemed to him an almost holy place, and he was shocked when I gave him my opinion that the fire in the Green Room had not been extensive, but had been used as a ploy to build a new theatre, which should not have required the destruction of the old. I told him how I had raced down from my digs on that fateful morning to inspect the damage, but did not mention that I had met Austin Clarke on the same mission. He was also fascinated to hear that I had been at the funeral of his dear friend, the painter Jack B. Yeats, in Herbert Street. But I did not mention that the boisterous Behan, seeing the solemn assembly in their mourning clothes outside the Peppercannister church, had saluted them cheekily, with a query of 'Head or harp?' as if they were street urchins playing pitch and toss.

Beckett was now deeply involved in the translations of his own works, an annoying but necessary procedure for someone of his exactitude. The South African writer Patrick Bowles had worked with him on *Molloy*, but found it daunting. Patrick said that Beckett would not accept any compromise in his relentless search for the right word. Especially hard were the jokes, which were scattered like raisins throughout the text. With his extraordinary command of both languages, Beckett couldn't rest until he had found an equivalent in the other tongue: he lived balanced between French and English, a bilingual bicycle. Because of his lengthy exile, he now spoke a pure Hiberno-English of a certain vintage, free of more recent slang, whereas his French, through his wartime need to survive, had grown less academic and more colloquial.

Beckett also encouraged me to contact Maurice Nadeau at *Les Lettres Nouvelles*, and would later recommend my poems to Jerome Lindon of Les Editions de Minuit. Altogether, it was the strained, serious conversation of *deux hommes des lettres*. And although we had two or three drinks, we remained careful and decorous in our exchanges.

The Irish Werewolf

The advent of Con Leventhal changed all that. The abbreviation of Cornelius to Con was a legend in literary Dublin: according to the wags in the pub, 'Con' was short for 'Continental', an indication of his cosmopolitan tastes instead of a mere diminutive. Or had it to do with the lettering on the face of Leventhal's parents' sweetshop, 'Con Leventhal Fectionaries'?

Con was an old Paris hand who had decided to spend his last years there, near his old friend: Beckett helped him find a billet on the Avenue Montparnasse, only a stone's throw away. Con was a small, delicate, determined Dublin Jew with a lame leg, a lover of

CHAPTER SEVEN

ladies and horses, and a drinker of the old school, who could keep going day and night without showing undue signs of wear.

I had already been impressed with Beckett's sense of discipline, the mornings for writing, phone calls and presumably correspondence between twelve and one, a light lunch, then afternoon meetings with Schneider or dark-avised Roger Blin; I sometimes glimpsed them conducting their theatrical business in neighbourhood cafés like the Raspail Vert. Then a few drinks with chosen confidants, *souper* with Suzanne, and so, presumably, to bed, unless his relentless insomnia was biting, and he might sally forth again; it had been late at night that I had seen him with Giacometti.

But the arrival of Con seemed to subvert all this discipline. Now, if we met, it would be Leventhal, as well as Peter Lennon (a young writer from Dublin earning his living as a cultural correspondent for *The Guardian*), or other stray Irish passing through, like Beckett's former student, Leslie Daiken, a Dublin Jew like Leventhal. It was as if, after a day as a normal French *écrivain*, Beckett was transformed into an Irish werewolf. And the dives were different – not the sombre formality of the Closerie, or the side bar of La Coupole – but the Falstaff, an old haunt of the 1920s where the barman remembered Hemingway, the Rosebud, which ran until near dawn, and an even more downmarket dive called Scott's, which had the louche atmosphere of an old whorehouse. Indeed, Sam and Con seemed to know a lot about the ladies of the evening. Although the brothels were officially closed, there were still to be seen, in dim streets in Montparnasse, ladies loitering with handbags at knee level. '*Bon soir, Con!*' they murmured, as the dapper old Dubliner passed slowly by, a formal but hilarious greeting, considering the pun in French.

This was a different Beckett, the cockatoo hairdo flaring as he ran excited hands over or through it, the brandy or whiskey flowing (you could not pay for a drink in his company), the severe face crinkling with laughter. Why this dramatic transformation? It was mainly the gently subversive genius of Con, with whom Sam could discuss old Dublin days at Trinity with rueful nostalgia, what an excluded Catholic like myself would wryly regard as 'Trinners' talk. I also provided a vague link with the University College Dublin contemporaries who had been his poetic pals, people like Denis Devlin and Brian Coffey, and his best friend, Thomas MacGreevy. And Peter Lennon was from Dublin, and shared Beckett's detestation of the more oppressive aspects of the new Irish state. When John McGahern's second book, *The Dark*, was banned, Beckett waxed indignant, convinced that our countrymen would never change in their reactionary philistinism: *Watt* had got the hammer in 1954, and *Molloy* in 1956. And when my collection of stories, *Death of a Chieftain*, got savaged by Patrick Kavanagh in an Irish periodical and I was contemplating a riposte, Beckett was emphatic: 'Don't answer them; they're not worth it!' But there was also his uneasiness at his increasing fame: after the Formentor prize that he had shared with Borges, loomed the Nobel, and in some weird way he wanted to be reassured that the home ground was still there, and liked the fellow feeling that our little Irish group provided, where local references did not have to be explained.

The exchanges between Con and Sam could be marvellously comic, like two old stand-up comedians. Late one night, Con and I were discussing love, with the leisurely wistfulness of two world-weary romantics, a conversation that clearly irritated Beckett profoundly, both intellectually and emotionally. The great head was heaving up and down, the exasperated sighs were proliferating, until Sam saw a chance to shove in his oar:

CHAPTER SEVEN

'No love,' he said with satisfaction. 'Only fuck!'

There was a startled silence, before Beckett moved in again, ignoring the shock on both our faces, especially Con's. Con might like the activity, but he rarely used bad language.

'Eat – drink – fuck,' Sam declared. 'That's all,' adapting, consciously or unconsciously, Eliot's famous lines in *Sweeney Agonistes*.

I saw Con slowly gather his wits about him, hunch his shoulders and begin gently but implacably to stalk his quarry. The dialogue between those two old friends, like an impromptu playlet, ran something like this:

CON (*playing his pal like a fish*): We've been friends for a long time, Sam.

SAM (*uneasy and puzzled*): Old friend. Oldest of friends.

CON: We go a long time back.

S: Very far back.

C: Then why wouldn't you speak to me once?

S (*agitated*): Always speak to you, Con. Always. Old friend. (*Repeated vehemently.*)

C: Yet you ignored me. You refused to see me.

S: Impossible! Oldest of friends! Always recognised Con. (*In his agitation, Sam speaks in the third person about himself, and is almost babbling.*)

C: You ignored me. I came into Harcourt Street railway station, and you hid behind one of those big neo-classical pillars.

S (*startled*): Behind a pillar, Con?

C: Yes. Behind a pillar. D'you remember the pillars in Harcourt Street? D'you remember the Harcourt Street station? D'you remember the line?

As in a trance, Beckett reeled off the names of the stations, a south

Dublin litany of now closed and forgotten halts: Harcourt Street, Ranelagh, Beechwood Avenue, Milltown, Churchtown, Dundrum, Carrickmines, Stillorgan, Leopardstown near his own early home, Foxrock. Con listened silently, then moved in for the kill.

C: So you know the station and you know the line?

S: Like the back of me hand. Travelled it morning and night, to and from Trinity. Leaving home, going home.

C: Yet you hid from me behind one of those Grecian pillars!

S: Behind a pillar, from you? (*His expression a study in confusion.*)

C: Yes, you hid behind a pillar in Harcourt Street railway station from me – with a woman. Yes! You, who deny love, hid from your oldest friend because you were with a woman.

Beckett was silenced, flummoxed. Then he perked up.

'You're right,' he said brightly, 'the woman from Dundrum. You also fancied her yourself. But she always got off half-way.'

*

While Beckett could be great company, and gravely humorous, there was no doubt that his view of the universe was gloomy, 'as bleak as the arsehole of a Siberian wolf', to quote my wife, Madeleine. So I never felt bad if I was in poor humour myself, and indeed things seemed to go better, even swimmingly, if I was despondent as well, with sometimes several minutes of sympathetic silence between our carefully phrased sentences. He kept recommending me to read Calderón's *La Vida es Sueño*, a key play for him which he almost consented to stage, and I often had the strong impression that, for him, our world was unreal, almost a dream, a cruel dream. And because it was such, the courtesies had to be observed, politeness

CHAPTER SEVEN

was all, and although as an adolescent he had spurned the Spartan politeness of Foxrock, that early regime served him well now, keeping the beasts at bay.

As I got to know him, I always tried to get my own complaints in first, knowing he would easily vanquish me in the woe stakes. There was one period where I was deeply depressed, and the black dog, or the blue devil as Burns calls it, had fastened its claws on my back. My marriage was not going well, my work was not going well, and I was plagued with insomnia. Pills were not working, and I was not really into counting sheep.

'So what,' I asked Sam, 'do you do, when things are not going well and you can't sleep?'

'I play the course at Carrickmines, the old and the new, all eighteen holes, one by one, in my head.'

'I can't play golf,' I cried.

'That's a handicap.'

I looked up, startled. He was smiling.

*

Again, we were discussing suicide, a subject to which I brought all a young man's romantically gloomy ardour. Beckett, however, seemed to have given the matter a lot of thought. Although he was of the select company of those who, like Sophocles, would prefer not to have been born, when I asked him if he ever thought of ending it, he replied brusquely, 'Out of the question. But I have thought of disappearance.' His best plan, he elaborated, was a boat with a hole in the bottom, to be dredged up by divers. Then a philosophic sigh. 'That's legally impossible too. The widow wouldn't inherit for seven years.'

Another time, we were comparing ailments, a favourite topic: his eyes were beginning to cloud with cataracts, and, although he had been quite a sportsman in his youth, playing rugby and cricket for Portora and Trinity, and even boxing, his physical faculties were declining. He no longer played tennis with Suzanne or Bill Hayter, and even walked more gingerly, afraid of blundering into things. And he had suffered all his life from embarrassing ailments, a mouthful of bad teeth, boils on his bum, and now near blindness, not helped by his earlier tendency to buy non-prescription spectacles from the local chemist. But he never indulged in self-pity, describing his loss of sight as banal compared to the agony of his master, Joyce.

Athletic prowess and poor health seemed to run in the Beckett family: he startled me once by saying that he now had two uncles with only one leg between them. He said it with the grimly cheerful humour that never seemed to fail him, and alas it was true. The Becketts had circulatory problems, and Uncle Jim, a rugby captain and champion swimmer, had had both legs amputated, while his Uncle Gerald, who had played rugby for Ireland, and scored a try in a win against Scotland at Lansdowne Road, ended up with a wooden leg. Which came first, the chicken or the leg; in other words, did such miseries come to Sam's silent call? He had been a hospital orderly after the war, and always ministered without complaint to friends in adversity. And he had watched at the deathbed of both his parents and his beloved brother Frank. So there was some justification for the savagery of his humour, which recalled Alba in his first novel, *A Dream of Fair to Middling Women*, when she goes around 'grousing an old Irish air: "Woe and pain, pain and woe / Are my lot, night and noon..."' But while Sam might have been as specialised in sadness as a keening Irish crone, one could

CHAPTER SEVEN

argue that, when the microcosm of his interior misery was mirrored in the larger cataclysm of the Second World War, he was finally able to slough off his Beladqua early self and come into his own.

The Blazing Boulevard

For the Irish male, getting drunk together seems a necessary preface to intimacy, and Sam was no exception to that national trait. One balmy 14th July, in the evening, I was sitting calmly on the terrace of the Sélect with Serge Fauchereau, a serious young French critic who was working on a study of modern American poetry. Suddenly Sam lurched by, clutching a lady, whom I recognised as Joan Mitchell, a distinguished American painter whom I had already met, and whose powerful abstracts we all admired. Sam spied me, and drew to a swaying halt at our table, grinning glassily. He was clearly already on the tear, that most un-French of rituals. (I had begun to understand, through observing my in-laws and friends, that while the French might drink more than most of us, it was to be absorbed slowly, and only immediately before, during, and directly after meals. The berserk quality of an Irish or Anglo-American bender was alien and even frightening to them.)

Nothing would do Sam but that I should accompany him. The Cricket, as Joan Mitchell kept calling my poor French friend, was also swept along, awed and astonished by our mad antics. I tried to stall our downward slide: since I already knew that Sam had a soft spot for the lady, something he kept confirming quite vigorously at the café table, why did they not move to some quiet hotel, instead of getting drunk with us on Bastille night?

'Where does one go to be alone?' cried Sam, ignoring the fact that he was surrounded by small *hotels du passage*, which must have been familiar to him in the past.

Indeed, that seemed to be the problem – his growing fear of being recognised, especially in his own *quartier*. Joan was clearly not pleased by his prevarications, and in a desperate effort to play Cupid, I suggested that they should come home with me, since Madeleine was away, and take over the studio, while I continued my evening with Serge with whom I was discussing recent poems by John Berryman, and the San Franciscans Snyder and Duncan.

But my helpful offer of a billet was brushed aside by an alcoholically ambivalent Sam, who led our tattered band in the direction of the usual watering holes, where Con and others were already lying in wait, celebrating the French national holiday in Irish fashion. Supper was scorned as the spirits cascaded, and we were all more than merry, except Joan Mitchell, who felt the evening had taken a wrong turn when Sam had sighted an Irish pal and used him as a diversion, a green herring. Joan was a famous drinker herself, so, after a few belts of Scotch, she lit into me and my French friend.

'Listen, Montague, do you always travel with your pet cricket?'

I tried to translate this for Serge, who could not quite see the connection between being a critic and a marsh-dwelling insect. It was all the more embarrassing because Serge was of small stature, although not of mind: he was the best-read Frenchman I had yet met.

'Don't you know, Montague, that critics are a low form of life, so low that they shouldn't be spoken to, only kicked in the butt? I never met a critic who knew his ass from his elbow, so there must be something wrong with you if you have to travel with a pet critic.'

Sam was enjoying the conversation, while trying to limit the damage; he must have had some experience of Joan on the warpath.

CHAPTER SEVEN

And Serge was grinning with pleasure, especially since I was translating only half of what was being said about him. Joan shifted her shotgun in my direction.

'Sam says that you're a poet. Do you think that you're a poet?'

I deflected this question as delicately as possible, murmuring the old Irish belief that it was an honour only others could bestow, and should not be claimed too loosely by oneself, or some such sententious sentiment.

'Okay, so Sam says you're a poet, but are you a *great* poet? I know I'm a great painter, or at least I feel so after I've finished a painting. But do you feel that you're a *great* poet?'

Sam had become visibly agitated, hurling his arms around, heaving his head, as he often did when in some distress (at a later stage he would sometimes retire totally into himself, like a mule or a mollusc). But now he seemed to be dimly aware that Joan was taking out her frustration on me with her implacable interrogation, which was all the more discomfiting because unfair: I understood that this was not the end to the evening that she had hoped for, but I *had* tried (twice) to assist their rendezvous. Beckett became as sober and clear as he could under the circumstances.

'It's all a question of age,' he said. 'John is still young, but I think he's working well. They only start to call you "great" when you're old, and nearing the graveyard. Before that, they don't even read you, so how would they know? It's all a matter of age, and so-called dignity: a tip of the cap to the corpse.'

The critic was delighted by this high-level literary exchange. Unaccustomed to such lethal draughts of spirits, he was moving in and out of consciousness, but his excitement at being with Beckett, and a famous painter whom he also admired, kept him almost on course. But Joan would not give up, determined to drive a wedge into the evening she had lost.

'What about Sam's poetry? Is that great poetry?'

I fielded that as well as I could. 'Well, it's a different kind of poetry from mine – more learned, more intellectual. Sam is better educated than me, went to better schools, so he knows much more. He learnt a lot from Pound and the Surrealists. But since he's here, why don't you ask him yourself, as you asked me?'

She swivelled her shotgun-gaze towards Sam and repeated the question, less sharply. But after a certain point in the evening Sam did not believe in lengthy intellectual exchange, and that point had now been reached.

'My poetry,' said Sam, 'my poetry.' And he began to giggle. 'My poetry is –' But he never finished the sentence, because he was lost in a bubble of giggles, which ended in a snort of laughter, and a mangled mutter of 'My poetry …' as his hands implored heaven. As a critical judgement it left us back at the starting post, and even Joan did not dare enquire further.

By this time we had reached the Falstaff, and dawn was beginning to break. Our exchanges, which had collapsed into listless half-sentences, were brought to a close when a large shadow fell across the door. The well-known French-Canadian painter, Riopelle, Joan Mitchell's partner, had come in search of her. There were some polite murmurs of upcoming exhibitions and shows, before Jean-Paul gathered in Joan as a bear might sweep in his mate. Con suggested another drink for the road, and as dawn finally broke, we tottered out of the last dive, the former *bordel* called Scott's, with baby-pink decor. I propped Beckett along, who propped Serge, while Leventhal mooched ahead, swinging wide his lame leg.

CHAPTER SEVEN

'Con's a great man,' said Sam admiringly, watching him steer a careful but unsteady path home.

We parted ways at the top of the Boulevard Raspail, and I managed to hoist my swaying companions down as far as the Boulevard St Jacques, sometimes taking the two sides of the road with us, not to speak of the wall. But the morning traffic was still light, and I succeeded in half-carrying, half-shuffling Beckett into his home quarters, before giving him a final leg up. Then I hauled Serge along our slumbering courtyard, and deposited him on the spare bed that I had offered to the reluctant lovers only a few hours before, although now, in the soft grey light of a Paris morning, it seemed aeons ago. In later years, Serge would describe it as one of the most extraordinary nights of his life.

A day afterwards, there was a brief but beautiful note through the post: 'Thanks for your help up the blazing boulevard.'

Even my disapproving spouse was impressed.

The Custom of the *Quartier*

And I was impressed by the politeness of the inhabitants of our *quartier*, which probably attracted someone with such a deep sense of privacy. Though he drank heavily himself, Sam was disturbed by certain kinds of flamboyant 'Oirish' drunkenness, like Brendan Behan or Peter O'Toole, both of whom were prone to descend on Paris and wreck all around them, like rugby supporters. O'Toole was an especial *bête-noire*, having played a large part in an Abbey production of *Godot*, which Beckett had not sanctioned. The etiquette of the *quartier* demanded that one should not intrude on other people's dialogue-in-progress. Thus, when the Irish writer Aidan Higgins and his wife passed through Paris on their way home from Spain, we found a place for them to stay, and I acted as his interpreter, since he had little French. But I left Aidan and his wife alone with Beckett, knowing well how easily Sam could be upset by too much social pressure.

This sense of decorum was deeply rooted in French artistic life: you did not barge in as you might in a raucous Dublin pub like McDaid's. Sometimes, in the mornings, I would shoot out to the Liberté, one of the three bars at the top of the Avenue du Maine, for a late morning *café* or *calvados*, and see Sartre at a corner table. Or around three o'clock, I would glimpse him taking a late lunch at La Coupole. If I went down to the kiosk by the Rotonde in Montparnasse, to buy my *Herald Tribune*, I would sometimes see his strange, small, intent figure, one eye narrowed behind those thick glasses, eagerly rifling through his early copy of *Le Monde*. But if I had not called on Simone, despite Nelson Algren's encouragement, why should I bother Jean-Paul?

People make their paths through a city the way animals do through a field, and I had grown up to recognise the determined little ley-lines that rabbits make on their way to and from their burrows, and the field where the hares lived, growing careless only when they emerged for their spring boxing matches. And cows, even bulls, usually kept to their territory, except when love horned in. So why should humans not preserve the same instinctive courtesy? One did not intrude unless there was a genuine reason.

So when Madeleine and I found a lonely Brassaï playing the pinball machines, we spoke to him, because he had recently been injured, bewildered by a new set of traffic lights on the Boulevard Raspail, and neighbourly concern seemed in order. He confided that it was his seventieth birthday, and since he seemed totally alone, we swept him off to dinner, where he entertained us with stories of old

CHAPTER SEVEN

Paris, his days with Henry Miller and the ladies of Montmartre. And in due course I went round with Hayter to see him, and admire the wonderful small sculptures he was doing then.

What was important was how the presence of the famous or gifted was taken for granted. At a lavish party given by Oonagh Guinness, mother of my friend Garech Browne, in her Paris flat, I became aware of the obsessed way in which one of the guests was gazing around him, in particular at a marvellous but strange-looking girl with a pronounced squint.

'Isn't she beautiful?' he repeated again and again. Clearly someone who disdained conventional ideals of beauty, since the young woman was surrounded by models from Oonagh's husband's *maison de couture*, tall, slender and vacuous. He looked as if he wanted to take a permanent impression of her, a kind of mental photograph. And when I asked who he was, I was told it was Man Ray.

The Beckett Family Band

Sam was amused by my stories about the founding of Claddagh Records, and liked Garech, whose mother he had met under one of her manifestations. And of course Luggala was one of the most beautiful parts of his beloved Wicklow. So, in due course, Garech decided that Claddagh should do a Beckett record, with the warm approval of its Speech Director (myself). We had a long distance hope that we might lure Beckett to record something himself, a hope which Garech transferred to me, since I lived round the corner from our man.

As I was gathering *The Faber Book of Irish Verse*, I had been reading Sam's poetry carefully, and could ask, with feigned inno-

142

cence, how one should speak 'Alba', or my own favourite, 'Gnome'. But I got short change. I understood his hesitations, since I had great difficulty in reading my own work before an audience, and could only force myself to perform for the always necessary shekels. It raised the perennial dispute about whether the author or an actor should read the poet's work, a subject on which my poetic generation held a unanimous opinion, whereas Sam seemed to be on the side of the actor. I persevered, but his reluctance was profound, and he would offer only stage directions. It seemed to me to amount to a superstition, as though he would lose a piece of his soul if his voice were captured, the way some cultures react to being photographed.

Meanwhile, back at the Dublin ranch, Garech was trying to comply with all of Beckett's exacting demands. Con Leventhal, of course, for the sleeve note, with a drawing by Arikha of Beckett with his spectacles pushed up high on his forehead, like racing goggles. And since there was no question of him reading anything himself (though I had continued to press hard for even a fragment), we were all old friends of the actor Jack McGowran, who was one of Beckett's favourite voices. Sam suggested a selection from his novels, because the plays had had a fair outing, but since he couldn't, wouldn't come to Dublin, Garech had to arrange a recording session in London. And though Sam had little or no appreciation of our involvement with Irish traditional music, Garech was glad to record the one and only performance of the Beckett Family Band, with cousin John on the harmonium, nephew Edward on the flute, and Sam, with mellow vigour, striking the gong, a sound he had probably heard for the first time as a young man at the Abbey Theatre.

Garech tried his sly best to conspire with our engineers to catch a whisper of Beckett's directions to Jack, but Sam was too wily a bird, making sure that all extraneous material and out-takes were destroyed, until not a murmur of him remained. From where did all this precision and exactitude come? Perhaps from some glimpse of his father's workroom, but he also had a version of what Sean Ó Riada claimed, perfect pitch, so that the least wrong note pained him. And where his work was concerned, he was stubborn to the point of mulishness. When I was still engaged in trying to lure him into vinyl immortality, to get him to read even the most minuscule of verses, he put down his glass and smiled, switching suddenly from English to French, saying, *'Je te vois venir'*: I see you coming.

After the recording had been done to his satisfaction, I saw a new aspect of Beckett, his impatience, as he harried Claddagh for the finished product. It took time, especially since we knew that any slip would anger the Master, not only the recording itself, but the reproduction of the Arikha drawing, and the splendid photograph on the cover, of a vigilant Beckett with his alter ego, Jack, both listening to Beckett's words, Jack's voice. The irony was that while Beckett did not want to be recorded, Garech hated being photographed, as well as being as perfectionist as Sam in his attention to detail. So I was dealing with two Protestant fusspots, who were also like coy maidens, one refusing to speak his own words while tolerating the camera, the other averting his head from the photographer's flash while hounding down the sound of the human voice. Sam had also decided that the delay was due to Hibernian laxity, and he gave out his usual spiel about the Irish, forgetting that I was connected with the company, until I brought box after box of records back with me from Ireland. It still seems to me one of the best speech records in existence, and a key to Beckett's own sense of his prose masterwork, which would serve as an unacknowledged guide for actors in the future. I do not think, however, that the Beckett Family Band could ever have made it on the road.

The Public Man

Jean Martin, the French actor, said that Beckett made it a practice not to appear for his own plays, but he usually showed the flag for the Irish contribution to the Théâatre des Nations, especially by the Abbey. He attended their production, for instance, of *The Countess Cathleen*. Indeed, he brought his wife as well, which was one of the few occasions that I met this sober, quiet woman, reputed to be death on spirits and addicted to herbal remedies. Sam's introduction was brief. As Madeleine and I were making the necessary theatrical small talk with him, I enquired about the presence or absence of his own spouse.

'She's here,' he said, and no more, indicating a silent figure by his side.

Madeleine leaped the awkward gulf with a few platitudes in French, but it was clear that Sam was too shy to be adept at formal greetings. He did break through the tiresome opening night social rituals when I began to inveigh against the slow plot and predictable Twilight rhythms of the early Yeats play.

'Wait until the end,' he cautioned. 'There are some beautiful lines that nearly save the play, when Yeats lets go. And remember, it was early; I've hidden mine out of sight.'

I was about to enquire what play he was speaking of, when he surprised me by launching into a sort of singsong, perhaps the kind of chanting he had heard from Yeats himself on the Abbey stage, when he was a student:

CHAPTER SEVEN

'The years like great black oxen tread the world,
And God the herdsman goads them on behind,
And I am broken by their passing feet.'

But Sam could put on a show if he had to. He came out loyally for Jack's one-man show in a large Paris theatre, the Théâtre Edouard VII. It was destined to fail, because neither Sam nor Jack were yet the cult figures they would later become, and also because what we now recognise as a typical Beckettian performance (one actor on an austere stage delivering a monologue) had not yet caught on for general audiences. Besides, it was in English, an hour and a half of fine gloomy prose, with Jack shuffling around, swathed in a long, shabby coat, an extended public version of our Claddagh record, I was glad to observe.

There was a well-fuelled reception afterwards, though, and, miracle of miracles, Sam was there at the end of a receiving line, not in his polo neck and corduroy jacket, but in a fairly swanky suit and tie, a contrast to his down-at-heel alter ego on the stage. Considering his almost pathological shyness, it was a considerable effort for him, and I watched in admiration as he bent to speak to some of the most boring society people in Paris. On the edge of the throng, I saw a distinguished English lady novelist, sitting, as I thought, disconsolately. Betrayed by the general mood of generosity, I thought she might like to meet Sam, so I led her to the top of the queue, proud to introduce one accomplished writer to another. I had forgotten, from previous cloudy meetings in London literary pubs like the George, that she had a tongue like an adder.

She tore into Beckett. She had been through the war too, and had seen people killed, but if she felt like him, she would have the decency to keep it to herself. His writing was a disgrace to humanity.

If she despaired about people the way he seemed to, she wouldn't write at all. He was doing the dirt on life.

It was obviously a well-rehearsed speech, and of a kind that Sam had heard before. He did not answer, but let his head droop, like a tired horse, and when the tirade had exhausted itself, he raised an imploring gaze.

'Where is Con?' he asked.

I hurried to fetch him, and he came to the rescue immediately. Olivia Manning was filling her glass and smirking.

'Sorry, John. I suppose you think that was bad of me, but I've wanted to do it for years, and you gave me the chance.'

I felt like shit warmed up, but Beckett never reproached me, or enquired who she was. Years later, in a biography of that amiable Oxford publisher, Dan Davin, I read how he detested Olivia Manning so much that when she died his only comment was that she had been 'poisoned, no doubt, by her own venom'. But Sam seemed to have a practised skill in dealing with those smaller sharks that cruise the literary waters, hoping to wound and feed off the larger fish. There are times I have longed for his detachment, as another scraggy failed writer injects sullen bile into what one had hoped would be a civil exchange.

Salute in Passing

In my more grandiose moments, I dreamt that I would be the young Irish writer who would carry on from these great men. But if the young Beckett was daunted by the Joyce of *Finnegans Wake* (his first public efforts in French were in that famous collaborative translation of the Anna Livia monologue), how much more difficult it would be to try to follow his trilogy as well! Besides, the great era of Modern experiment seemed to be over, especially in prose. I managed a creditable book of stories, which Sam said he liked, especially the title story, an extravaganza set in the south of Mexico, 'Death of a Chieftain', because it was the most experimental. And translations of my poems were also leaking into the more prestigious journals, and getting some notice. I was reviewing, as well, for *Le Monde* and *La Quinzaine Littéraire*, usually discussing my Irish contemporaries like McGahern and the more erratic Higgins, as well as Clarke, Kavanagh and Kinsella, to create a French context for the newer Irish writing. It was almost a weakness of mine, dreaming a family to compensate for the one I had only briefly had.

But poetry, it was finally becoming clear, was my real passion. And something that had become depressingly obvious to me was that Sam no longer read much poetry, even modern French poetry. After all, he had been introduced by Rudmose Brown at Trinity to his French contemporaries, and had worked for a while on Jouve. The perfervid imagination of Jouve, his heady brew of sensuality, Catholicism and psychoanalysis, might no longer appeal to the often ascetic Beckett, but for someone of my Catholic background of incense, purity and ritual punishment, it was still fascinating. Beckett had also translated Eluard for the little magazine *This Quarter*, poems reproduced in his friend George Reavey's anthology, *Thorns of Thunder*, which I had found in the library of the Royal Dublin Society. And Char had been a Resistance leader in the Vaucluse, not far as the crow flies from Roussillon, where Beckett had found refuge: I made a kind of pilgrimage to Char at his home near the beautiful village of Isle-sur-Sorgue, with its slowly turning water wheel. And squat Guillevic, ironic Frenaud, and their friend Follain, could be seen traipsing through the streets of Paris after some literary *soirée* where the wine had flowed: Follain was killed crossing a street near the Louvre.

So while Beckett's interest in modern French poetry was lapsing, I was beginning to believe that it was far more exciting and varied than anything recent in English, with its strong philosophical undertone which impressed my intellectually hungry mind. The only more recent poet Sam had translated was Alain Bosquet, which I reproached him for, since Bosquet was mainly a journalist, but Sam simply said he was a 'pal', which seemed to excuse everything. As for my own pals, Esteban, Bonnefoy, Deguy, Dupin, Fourcade, Marteau, he seemed never to have heard of them; *le bande à Beckett*, Beckett's gang, was mainly connected with the theatre and the *nouveaux romans* of Les Editions de Minuit.

I was given a chance, however, to offer affection and homage to my great compatriot and neighbour. One must remember that the French did not fall head over heels with joy when Beckett received the Nobel, which Malraux had been expecting; Mauriac was also prone to make sour comments about this incomprehensible import. However, the *Magazine Littéraire* asked me to write a long piece on Beckett, upon which I and Madeleine slaved for a summer. So I found myself in the company of admirers like Blin and Ionesco (from the theatre), and Alain Robbe-Grillet, Claude Mauriac and Claude Simon, briefly joining *la bande à Beckett*. Sam liked the essay himself, particularly because it also placed him in an Irish, or even a Trinity College, tradition, of Swift, Goldsmith, Berkeley and Synge, names not always bandied around the Sorbonne and Saint-Germain.

Rombaldi, the French publishing house for which Madeleine was now working, had a plan to reproduce this essay, which had covered both the Irish and French bases, in a combined French and New

York English-language edition commemorating the Nobel literary prizes. But Barney Rosset of the Grove Press was dog-in-the-mangerish about this plan, which was a pity, because the French edition was handsomely produced and printed, again with drawings by Arikha. But the kind of sour nemesis which stalks great writers struck again, with a blandly hostile introduction by a member of the Swedish Academy, which made it clear that he was not a Beckett fan.

Meanwhile, inspired by my surroundings, I was trying to write in French myself, muttering lines as I marched the streets. But I was beginning to realise that it was not only Sam who had lost interest in contemporary poetry, but the whole French nation, and that this indifference to poetry might always have been a national characteristic, except during periods of crisis, as when poetry was part of the Resistance. 'Poetry is a pastime,' says Alceste in Molière's *Le Misanthrope*. And although the context is comic, it finds an echo in Baudelaire's sombre reflection, '*La France a horreur de la poésie*'. It was not part of their lives, even in the raging outcast manner of a Kavanagh, or the solemn intoning of Clarke in his weekly poetry programme on Radio Eireann. The French equivalents as public personalities, keepers of the flame, the tribal conscience, were now the prose writers, the *causeries* of Sartre, the *bloc-notes* of François Mauriac. Only Cocteau had a public face, and his poetry seemed lightweight compared to the great poets of the period, like Jouve, Char and Ponge. Prévert was also read, because he was simple, and could be sung. But my French poetic contemporaries had to be content with tiny editions of two hundred or so, mainly *service de presse*, a matter of prestige for publishing houses, unless and until they weathered indifference long enough to reach the pocket book stage.

*

Two later anecdotes would come to crystallise and symbolise my increasing disaffection with the French attitude towards poetry. A distinguished novelist from Brittany, Michel Mohrt, was a regular visitor to Ireland, and observing the public success of my long poem, *The Rough Field*, recommended it to his own publishing house, Gallimard. A surprised Deguy was part of the reading committee, and piled in behind the proposal, only to have it turned down by the boss himself, who picked up the book, and, discovering it was written in verse, placed it aside, declaring, '*Mais, c'est de la poésie! Ca vend pas.*'

And years later, when Deguy and other French friends had assembled my *Selected Poems* in French, it was recommended by Beckett to Lindon of Les Editions de Minuit, which had been founded as a Resistance publishing house. Lindon turned it down for the same reason as Gallimard, his clinching argument being that even Sam's poetry didn't sell. If I was to have a future as a poet, it was clearly not going to be in France, from which I had already unconsciously begun to beat a retreat.

CHAPTER EIGHT

DANCE ON, DANCE ON
or
A Rose for George

Shortly after my first, very slim, volume, *Forms of Exile*, appeared in 1958, I got a very friendly note from Theodore Roethke 'with the admiration of an old party'. His response was probably prompted by our mutual friend, the American visionary painter Morris Graves, but it was pleasant all the same for a novice to receive. I was twenty-nine, but poets grew up more slowly in those thorny days; the garden was wild and difficult.

    I already knew and admired Roethke's work, with its strong lyric thrust, so unusual in contemporary American poetry: had Dylan Thomas not asked to meet him on one of his wearing lecture tours? I had begun to read Roethke when I was a Teaching Assistant at Berkeley, in a Department that was academically strong but not awash with enthusiasm for poetry. For nourishment I listened to Kenneth Rexroth fulminating on Sunday mornings on KPFA, the local intellectual radio station, but Robert Duncan and Jack Spicer were away on the East Coast, and Allen Ginsberg had only just slouched towards the Bay Area to be reborn. And even though Gary Snyder was back from his pilgrimages in rural Japan, at sea, or in a Zen monastery, he had not yet become a major presence on the local

CHAPTER EIGHT

poetry scene, a scene still in embryo though it would soon burst forth, all its elements suddenly cohering in a kind of orgiastic glory.

Whereas Roethke's plangent music brought me back to the traditional lyric, with a post Freudian lilt, Yeats in the speakeasy:

> The whiskey on your breath
> Could make a small boy dizzy;
> But I hung on like death:
> Such waltzing was not easy.

Was I moved by memories of my own father, in Rodney Street, Brooklyn? I seemed to see the calloused hand of a hard-worked man, hear the scraping of a fiddle, perhaps my Uncle John, or Eddie Montague, playing as the drunks were tossed down the tenement stairs and the women wrung their hands:

> We romped until the pans
> Slid from the kitchen shelf;
> My mother's countenance
> Could not unfrown itself.
>
> The hand that held my wrist
> Was battered on one knuckle;
> At every step you missed
> My right ear scraped a buckle.

Was a gangster called Garland shot in our kitchen? Had my father really been found out cold in the morgue, his forehead creased from a car accident? What I remembered more than anything else, beyond the roar of the El and the confusions of the period, was his caress:

> You beat time on my head
> With a palm caked hard by dirt,
> Then waltzed me off to bed
> Still clinging to your shirt.

And like myself Ted had known the spell of childless old women, 'These nurses of nobody else… (who) plotted for more than themselves.' I could be back in my restoring Garvaghey home with my aunts when I read lingering lines like:

> … they picked me up, a spindly kid,
> Pinching and poking my thin ribs
> Till I lay in their laps, laughing,
> Weak as a whiffet;
> Now when I'm alone and cold in my bed,
> They still hover over me,
> These ancient leathery crones…

But it was not all simple child's-eye memories of growth in a green place, Saganaw, Michigan, or Garvaghey, County Tyrone. I had bought a copy of Roethke's *The Waking* (1953) which had won the Pulitzer prize, with a brooding portrait of the beetle-browed poet on the cover. And already a beat of madness could be heard in the slow ominous lines of the title poem, a villanelle, frightening in its fierce control:

CHAPTER EIGHT

> We think by feeling. What is there to know?
> I hear my being dance from ear to ear.
> I wake to sleep, and take my waking slow.

Here was a poet who was determined to go the whole hog, dense with physical memories of the soiling of childhood, full of little comforting cries and invocations against the dark powers, and seeking aid and example from the greatest, Dante to Wordsworth.

> Dante attained the purgatorial hill,
> Trembled at hidden virtue without flaw,
> Shook with a mighty power beyond his will, –
> Did Beatrice deny what Dante saw?

Seeking indeed that cosmic dance of unity glimpsed by Sir John Davies and celebrated by Yeats as his supreme symbol; was it still possible in our time?

> Is that dance slowing in the mind of man
> That made him think the universe could hum?

By the time his *Words for the Wind* came out in England in 1958, I was newly married and back working in Dublin. I loved the disgusting little songs for children because, although he never had any, Roethke could enter immediately into their natural naughtiness, unfulfilled by laundered Mother Goose rhymes. Perhaps 'The Cow' had special meaning for me, since I had tried to learn how to milk in our warm, wood-stalled byre, and been slapped across the face for my lack of skill by an urgent, fecund mother.

There Once was a Cow with a Double Udder.
When I think of it now, I just have to Shudder!
She was too much for One, you can bet your Life:
She had to be Milked by a Man and his Wife.

But the new note was a sequence of love poems, lyrical with delight, but again with a Yeatsian undertow. Trying to live through the same experiences myself, I was troubled by their heavily literary references, all the way back to Tudor times, the lovesick pursuits of Wyatt and Sidney, so closely woven that, although the lines extolled love, I could not catch sight of a flesh and blood beloved through the thicket of words. I did not believe, any more than Joyce Kilmer, that my love was 'sweeter than a tree' but I could recognise the obsession, and the need to fulfil onself with another, the greatest adventure possible to us in this life or any other:

> I kiss her moving mouth,
> Her swart hilarious skin;
> She breaks my breath in half;
> She frolicks like a beast;
> And I dance round and round,
> A fond and foolish man,
> And see and suffer myself
> In another being, at last.

From Morris Graves and his friend Richard, I learnt that Roethke had married a beautiful young woman called Beatrice O'Connell, of Irish background, presumably, although she was a Bennington girl from Virginia. For Morris and Richard, he was the Poet, a larger than life-size figure, balanced on the edge of excess. So I was not

CHAPTER EIGHT

surprised when I received a wild piece, 'The Old Florist's Lament', a Yeatsian ballad about his Prussian father, sent from some nursing home on 19th February 1959. With neighbours like Brendan Behan and Patrick Kavanagh, I was ready for anything in the line of eccentricity, but I was taken aback by the vehemence of this 'Slight Song in Dubious Taste':

> Who but a Prussian hog could know,
> Or a sleek Polish ham,
> Stettin's a place so cold and wet,
> Pork keeps in good supply.
> A cold-eyed, drunken Prussian man
> Taught Jews new ways to die.

In the summer of 1960 I had a further note from Roethke, announcing his arrival in Ireland with his beloved, Beatrice. He was not staying at Morris Graves's lordly Woodtown Manor, but in a small private hotel, which boded well for his Dublin visit because it placed him in the centre of a Dublin just beginning to come alive again, with architects, poets and painters, a circle of gaiety into which he was quickly drawn. Michael Scott, our leading architect, who was designing the new Abbey Theatre, threw a big party for him, where Roethke distinguished himself by approaching a lady from both ends of her dress, a vigorous salutation not altogether common in Ireland. She took it in good part, since her husband was engaged in a less lethal version of the same approach at the other side of the room. But there was another side to Roethke than these antics of a roaring boy.

It was a red letter day when he came round to see me in our basement flat in Herbert Street. Having resigned from Bord Failte,

DANCE ON, DANCE ON

I was working on my second book, *Poisoned Lands,* and copies of many of the poems were spread across our only table. And he had brought some of the beautiful nature meditations which would form part of his 'North American Sequence', lamentations suddenly leavened by exultation, the long moody line of Whitman taking over from Yeats, a movement more natural to his ebullient American self:

> On the Bullhead, in the Dakotas, where the eagles eat well,
> In the country of few lakes, in the tall buffalo grass at the base of the clay buttes,
> In the summer heat, I can smell the dead buffalo,
> The stench of their damp fur drying in the sun,
> The buffalo chips drying.
>
> Old men should be explorers?
> I'll be an Indian.
> Ogalala?
> Iroquois.

It was heady stuff of a kind I was not really used to in Ireland, a young poet and a veteran exchanging verses across a table. While I had many friendly acquaintances among the Irish writers, writing itself, like lovemaking, was a private occupation, and craft was rarely discussed in the way Roethke did, praising the four beat lines in some of my newer poems, and the attempted use of a refrain. I remember also that quite a few adverbs went to the wall: he thought they made the tempo of a poem sluggish. It was my first experience since the Iowa workshop of this workmanlike approach to the process of poetry, although in Iowa I had not been lucky enough to

CHAPTER EIGHT

be taught by a master. I was so pleased that I suggested we should go together to visit Mrs Yeats.

When I made the suggestion, I was ignoring some storm signals. After our session in Herbert Street, Roethke produced a hip flask from his back pocket, the contents of which cascaded down his throat, after he had anxiously warned me not to tell Beatrice. I had nothing against drink, in fact was in favour of it, at the right time, as relaxation in good company. But Ted's application to it had begun to seem to me reckless and lacking in ceremony. I suggested that we should repair to a pub and have a few celebratory and companionable pints, but he was afraid Beatrice would not like that, though I proposed we call her up to join us in Phil Ryan's in Baggot Street, where Liam Miller might drop in on his way home from the Dolmen Press. He had already met the bearded Miller, and they had taken to each other mightily, but he seemed still afraid of the easy exposure of a pub, serious talking with glasses in hand and maybe a song in the background, although that would change when he got to Inisboffin Island.

Meanwhile, he was distracted by my wife's return from work, and that good Frenchwoman was politely startled by the way in which, with little ado, he managed to pay manual homage to her bottom, in other words, to grab her ass. I hustled him up the stairs, and pointed him home, towards Leeson Street and his waiting Beatrice.

'Don't tell her,' he muttered again.

We met next afternoon at the top of Dawson Street, outside a florist's. The idea, of course, was Ted's, since even the writing Irish were not literate in the language of flowers. But for Mrs Yeats, only the best would do, and when the shopgirl produced a conventional bouquet, her offering was greeted with not-so-friendly roars of disparagement.

'When I say flowers,' Roethke growled, 'I mean real flowers, not limp, dead stalks, ready for the garbage. Christ Jesus, I was reared in a greenhouse!'

The assistant cowered, and I cowered with her.

'I'm going to see a lady, a great lady, a specialist in spooks! Have you ever heard of the poet Yeats, and his wife, George?'

The poor girl was clearly not a great scholar of poetry, so I interposed on her behalf. 'We are going to see an old friend of mine, the poet's widow. Perhaps we could see some roses?'

'Yeah! Roses! Let's see some roses!' roared Roethke from behind me. 'Real roses, not these dying, crumpled things! Bring me your best! I know everything there is to know about roses.'

And indeed he did. And would celebrate them in that wonderful poem, 'The Rose':

> And I think of roses, roses,
> White and red, in the wide six-hundred-foot greenhouses,
> And my father standing astride the cement benches,
> Lifting me high over the four-foot stems, the Mrs Russells, and his own elaborate hybrids,
> And how those flowerheads seemed to flow toward me, to beckon me, only a child, out of myself.

The manager was called, and the matter was settled by Roethke and him descending into the basement or bowels of the shop to choose a basket of flowers, mainly roses. Indeed, the two men stood together, discussing the language of roses, the damask for love, the white-and-red for England, the tea rose for constancy, and, of

CHAPTER EIGHT

course, the whole garland as crown. Even Roethke seemed mollified, but he was still fussing as we hovered on the pavement outside.

'Do you think we got it right, John? Is there anything else she might like, besides flowers?' And then the leading question, 'Does Mrs Yeats drink?'

He swayed anxiously on the footpath like an outsize Red Riding Hood, swinging his basket of flowers. He was nervous as a kitten, or a swain on a first date, and badly in need of fortification, which I thought better not to seek out; Mrs Yeats had said that she wasn't feeling her best, and the idea of the two of us turning up late and bombed on her doorstep did not appeal to me. When I assured him that she did take a drop, he was relieved, but he was less happy when I directed him to that fashionable shop, Smyths of the Green, to buy a bottle of Bristol Cream.

'Sherry! Good God, she drinks sherry! I don't know anyone that drinks stuff like that! That's for old ladies!'

Which of course she was; we hailed a taxi by the Traitors Arch and left for Rathmines, the bouquet between us with the nozzle of the bottle protruding among the flowers like a gangster's gat. But when we reached the gate, and steps up to her late Victorian house, he was still in a tizzy; all those years of studying Yeats were fizzing in him like champagne.

'Is this her house? Did Yeats ever live here himself?'

As the bell rang and rang in the depths of the house, Ted became more agitated, taking out the bottle to swing in his left hand, while he held up the flowers in the other. Finally I heard Mrs Yeats shuffling towards the door, which opened slowly, all the more because the carpet had got curled into it.

'Hello, John,' said George Yeats, and bent to smooth it with her left hand. The wait was all too much for the tense Roethke, who now shot out his right hand in greeting.

'Mrs Yeats, I brought you some flowers!' he bellowed, whereupon she straightened her back, scattering most of them across the floor.

'Hmph!' she said, a cross between a hoot of dismay and a cry of astonishment, and turned to disappear in the direction of the kitchen.

'What's wrong? What's happened?' cried Ted, as we gathered the scattered flowers from the floor. 'Is she coming back? Did we upset her?'

When she came back she was carrying a vase, and she began to beam with pleasure as Roethke tidied the flowers into it.

'Roses! A whole garland! How nice of you. Poor Willy's favourite flower, the only ones he could recognise. He was nearly colour blind, you know.'

As we helped her select a spot for them in the sitting room, she explained that she was not feeling well, and could not guide us through the library. Sensing a companion in misery, Roethke detailed his own health problems, and soon they were discussing cures for arthritis, the relationship between rheumatism and climate, the Pacific Northwest being nearly as rainy as Ireland. He offered to rub her back as she stretched on a couch, but she accepted a glass of sherry instead. Soon they were at ease, gossiping about critics and poetic contemporaries. One English poet-critic who had bored her got short shrift.

'He keeps sending me his absurd books. As a critic he may have some place in a university, but as a poet he is intolerable!'

Her vehemence delighted Roethke. 'I've been thinking of the

CHAPTER EIGHT

right word for that fella for years. And intolerable hits the nail right on the head. He's dry as a bone in the desert.'

It was clear they had taken to each other, and I left to wander into the library. In due course, I was joined there by a, for once, totally contented Roethke. I showed him some of the mystical notebooks with designs elaborate as geometry, or higher algebra, and he was boyishly impressed. He had simmered down to a thoughtful quietness, his best mood, as when we were looking together at the poems. We said goodbye to Mrs Yeats, who was nearly asleep; Ted tucked the rug around her, with great tenderness.

Instead of going back to his hotel and my home, I brought him to a large, comfortable public house in Rathmines, which I sometimes frequented on my way to and from the Public Library. I ordered a slowly drawn pint of Guinness, but before it had arrived with its priestlike collar of froth, Roethke had already sunk two large whiskeys, and called for a third. It seemed a good time to be serious. I asked him why he drank in the haphazard way he did, and said I found it hard to reconcile the two Roethkes, the sensitive poet and the other, the roaring boy whose heart somehow did not seem in it. He hunched his large shoulders, and his domed head glistened with nervous sweat.

'I drink like this,' he said, 'because I'm afraid of death. It's all I seem to think about.'

The dark mood passed, and by the time I brought him back he was ready to berate Beatrice for not being a medium like George Yeats. In a few days Ted and Beatrice would leave for the west, and Richard Murphy's Inisboffin Island. I planned to catch up with them there, but by the time I got to the island, Roethke was in Ballinasloe Hospital. A plan to produce his later work from the Dolmen Press in Dublin was abandoned, although its putative title,

DANCE ON, DANCE ON

Dance On, Dance On, revived the Yeatsian dream of unity in the dance. On Inisboffin he had discovered the company of drinkers and pub singers; there was very little else to do on the island for long periods. But something about that Ireland was also dangerous for the euphoric side of his temperament; songs like 'Gob Music' were nearly in as bad taste as 'The Florist's Lament':

> Indeed I saw a shimmering lake
> Of slime and shining spit,
> And I kneeled down and did partake
> A bit of the likes of it.
> And it reminded me – But Oh!
> I'll keep my big mouth shut.

In three years Roethke would be dead, and the marvellous poems he showed me would be published posthumously. The travail of that generation of American poets is now well documented, although the reasons for it are still not really clear. The loneliness of the poetic vocation is a constant, exacerbated by the indifference of that vast country, whereas there is always some kind of context in Ireland, however rough and residual. That is perhaps what Roethke glimpsed in Dublin and Inisboffin; Ireland may be the last place in the English speaking world where the title *poet* has some authority, and Roethke would have loved to participate in such a community. His melancholy 'Saginaw Song' describes the constricting gentility of his Midwestern background:

> In Saginaw, in Saginaw,
>   There's never a household fart,
> For if it did occur,

CHAPTER EIGHT

It would blow the place apart, –

Whereas he dreamt himself a beloved bard, performing before an admiring audience:

> O, I'm the genius of the world, –
> Of that you can be sure,
> But alas, alack, and me achin' back,
> I'm often a drunken boor;
> But when I die – and that won't be soon –
> I'll sing with dear Tom Moore,
> With that lovely man, Tom Moore.

Then there was the pattern of drinking during that period. No one from Ireland can afford to cast a stone, but there was a madness to the martini mystique, those cocktail parties where guests guzzled 'highballs' – often pure spirit – all night long, even during the meal. Americans of the time considered their cocktail culture sophisticated, but in its way it was as primitive a ritual as the proof of masculinity through the consumption of pints in the student pubs of Dublin. And it was more dangerous because less passive: the object was to stimulate the brain cells, dissolve the inhibitions, rather than ease them. And there were the fantasies hard liquor feeds: Roethke's father was a strict German, not a wild drunk, and his son probably had not run with gangsters:

> A place I surely did like to go
> Was the underbelly of Cicero…

While American poets have found shelter in the academies, there is something artificial in this arrangement, like seeking sanctuary during the medieval plagues; what about real life, as they say? French poets, like Frenaud and Guillevic, earned their living as civil servants, while there is a long tradition of poets in the diplomatic service, such as Pablo Neruda and Octavio Paz from Latin America, Claudel and St Jean Perse from France, and Denis Devlin from Ireland. Besides, English departments are often hostile and uncomprehending; however scholarly a poetic interloper may be, they find it hard to take him or her seriously unless the poet bears and wears the insignia of serious scholarship, like T.S. Eliot. Creative Writing classes have eased this artificial division between creator and explicator, but Roethke was a pioneer in those early days of the poetry workshop, and still believed in being a scholar of the poetic tradition.

Then, both Robert Lowell and Roethke had massive personal problems into which it would be presumptuous to pry. Ted was one of those large but gentle men who lived at the extremes of existence, his anguish and ecstasy fused only in the furnace of the lyric. He tried to play the athlete as well as the poet, a two fisted drinker who identified with the minute, and the helpless, as in his delicate poem to 'The Meadow Mouse':

> But this morning the shoe-box house on the back porch is empty.
> Where has he gone, my meadow mouse,
> My thumb of a child that nuzzled in my palm? –
> To run under the hawk's wing,
> Under the eye of the great owl, watching from the elm-tree,
> To live by courtesy of the shrike, the snake, the tom-cat.

CHAPTER EIGHT

> I think of the nestling fallen into the deep grass,
> The turtle gasping in the dusty rubble of the highway,
> The paralytic stunned in the tub, and the water rising, --
> All things innocent, hapless, forsaken.

Above all, there was that fierce competitiveness, the need to be number one, which raged throughout that generation like a virus, as if poetry were a form of prize fighting, and they were all vying to be heavyweight champion. Fame is the spur, indeed, but one should not rowel Pegasus. I sometimes fear that Irish poetry has been infected with this self seeking attitude, to its potential detriment. Lowell was the culprit, with his power mania: when Berryman was completing (I almost wrote *competing*) the *Dream Songs* in Dublin, Lowell wrote to him, saying that his Irish poems – which are not his best – made Berryman 'the best Irish poet since Yeats'. Wilful lines he was later to use about Seamus Heaney, although there is no evidence that Lowell had ever bothered to read Clarke or Kavanagh, let alone Kinsella or myself, or indeed any contemporary Irish poetry in either language, before he put the skunk among the pigeons.

Whereas Roethke on the far Pacific coast had done his homework; his notes to me were garnished with generous postscripts, 'Say hello to Kavanagh' or, more surprisingly, because he had published so little, 'Give my best to (Padraic) Fallon.' And his class notes showed that he had introduced his students to contemporary Irish poetry, and, according to his biographer, Allan Seager, 'Even in London, Ted had not fallen into a literary circle he liked better.' I believe he glimpsed in Ireland a community where he might have prospered, but it was too late, and it only drove him mad again. Later in the decade John Berryman would arrive to live and work

DANCE ON, DANCE ON

for a longer period against the same backdrop. My last communication from Roethke was a sad, small, Blakean lyric of travail wrought into a healing sweetness. It was on a small card, surprisingly tinselled with stars:

> In a hand like a bowl
> Danced my own soul,
> Small as an elf,
> All by itself.

CHAPTER NINE

PASSAGE TO CALIFORNIA

I
On the Way

Looking back now, I can see that my life during the early 1960s had a main plot, my attempt to come to terms with my wife's France, and a subplot, to become my own man in my own right (or write), which seemed, increasingly, to involve being elsewhere. The first and major temptation was Berkeley and the Bay Area, with which I first formed a connection in the mid-1950s, and where I came back to teach in the mid-1960s, at the height of the campus turbulence.

I first came to Berkeley in September 1955, after a long hot summer in Mexico with Madeleine. It had been a very literary tour: I took Graham Greene's *The Lawless Roads*, D.H. Lawrence's *The Plumed Serpent*, and Malcom Lowry's *Under the Volcano*, as our guides. Lowry led us to mescal, D.H. Lawrence to the bull ring and the stone temples, Graham Greene to the Gulf of Mexico, where a bored official took us off a little tramp steamer travelling to Yucatan, a potentially dangerous journey for two naïve *gringos* like ourselves. Instead, we travelled by bus southwards through the night, trying to sleep next to a gobble of turkeys. We passed through San Antonio Tuxtala, where a cluster of local men, some bearing machetes, began to pester Madeleine and myself as we tried to swallow our soup. Fleeing to the bus, we tried to dismiss it as a nightmare, but I learnt

CHAPTER NINE

later that a stray Irishman had been killed there. But we found our favourite Mexico south of Oaxoca in the Isthmus of Tehuantepec, staying in a decrepit luxury hotel which later gave me the background for the title story of *Death of a Chieftain*. I also began to read Octavio Paz's *Piedra del Sol*, Sun Stone, which seemed to capture that many-layered land:

> voy por tu cuerpo como por el mundo,
> tu vientre es una plaza soleada,
> tus pechos dos iglesias donde oficia
> la sangre sus misterios paralelos...

I loved Mexico, but one must live, and I had a job as teaching assistant at the University of California at Berkeley. We travelled back up the spine of Mexico, through Los Angeles to Santa Barbara, where Madeleine's aunt-in-law, Madame Coste, had a ranch. We were met at the bus station not by the aunt-in-law, but by the youngest, and most formidable-looking, of Madeleine's blood aunts, *Tante* Christiane d'Avoust, who was studying photography in Santa Barbara, and hoping to break into films. Christiane was not well-favoured, but she was indomitable, not to say fierce. There had been a forest fire, and the hills around Santa Barbara were burning, with the air smelling of scorched branches, but she ignored it all, rattling on about the family while barrelling us on to the Coste ranch.

Madame Coste was a raddled monster, my first encounter with French anti-semitism as she railed against Mendès-France and the treaty negotiations with Indochina: '*un petit juif qui veut vendre la France*', 'a little Jew who wants to sell France'. She was a weird blend of intolerance and prurience: for the first time in nearly a year, Madeleine and I were put in separate rooms, so we had to meet each other, for carnal disport, among the grazing Longhorns. A few days later, Christiane drove us up to San Francisco by the coast road, Highway No. 1. That it had been declared 'Closed', blocked by falling boulders, mattered nothing to her as she urged her little Citroen onwards, announcing that she had driven through the jungles of Indochina, and that a few panicky Americans would not stop a d'Avoust from showing us the most beautiful part of California.

After Madeleine had helped me find a room, we bade a tearful farewell at the bus station as she left for Chicago and the University of Illinois. But why had I been chosen for the prestigious graduate school at Berkeley? The answer came a few days later when Tom Parkinson, all six foot seven of him, swept into the teaching assistants' room. 'Where is Montague?' he growled, and explained that I was going to work with him for the year, a year during which I would discover what he called 'the California branch of glorious poetry', decide to get married, and decide to go home. If I had absorbed the Existentialist view that one creates one's life by a series of choices, Berkeley was certainly a crossroads for me.

My choices were rendered all the more complicated because I began to love Berkeley. For a little Ulster Catholic boy, it was glorious to stride through the warm campus as the campanile struck, like the bells of Armagh Cathedral, but above flowering trees and lightly-clad students. The graduate school was tough, but it was there, in the Bay Area, again through Parkinson, that I discovered a living poetic community, of which he had been a part during his own youth. On the campus, however, he was known as a Yeats scholar, and, being Irish and a budding poet, I represented some

CHAPTER NINE

kind of complicated recompense for the other, wilder life he had abjured.

There is something magical and inevitable in one's choice of friends, as there is in one's choice of loves, and I was haunted by the memory of coming on an early poem of his, 'September Elegy', years before in a copy of *Horizon*. Tom was acting as a kind of poetic Fifth Column inside what the more intellectually severe Berkeley professors had dubbed 'the Harvard of the West'. He was Allen Ginsberg's academic advisor, for instance, and we would walk down from Parkinson's house in the hills to Ginsberg's cottage in Milvea, where Allen was rooming with Phil Whalen and some other wandering bards, whom I would slowly get to know as well. With his dark eyes enlarged behind thick spectacles, Allen looked rabbinical and was nearly as ill at ease in an academic discussion of Anglo-Saxon as I was. He was considering taking an MA degree at Berkeley, but, like myself, he would find the academic requirements too confining. In a way the Berkeley English Department did us both a service, by forcing us to recognise our priorities.

I moved from boarding house to boarding house in Berkeley, before ending up in Parkinson's basement. In the first of them I experienced an earthquake: I was sitting in my room one evening, trying to study either my Anglo-Saxon verbs or the early American novel, when the wall began to dance. 'Jesus, Mary and Joseph!' I cried, reverting to origins, and almost began a decade of the rosary. But that physical tremor was slight compared to the psychic earthquake of my first big Berkeley poetry reading.

Parkinson appeared at the door one evening to sweep me off to the Gallery Six, for either the first or the second public reading of *Howl*. A bow-tied Kenneth Rexroth was acting as MC; I had already heard one of his jazz and poetry performances in a San Francisco night club. The evening began quietly, with Phil Whalen murmuring his tranquil, intricately-structured verses. Meanwhile in the background, a stocky figure was collecting quarters to buy enormous jugs of 'Mountain Burgundy', which we drank from paper cups; I was told afterwards that it was Kerouac. Then Ginsberg stood up, and I heard a different Allen from the shy, shrewd student of Anglo-Saxon. He began quietly, but his voice lifted into incantation as he came to the Moloch passages, an apocalyptic vision of the tall towers of San Francisco, written under the influence of hallucinogens:

'Moloch whose eyes are a thousand blind windows! Moloch whose skyscrapers stand in the long streets like endless Jehovahs! Moloch whose factories dream and croak in the fog! Moloch whose smokestacks and antennae crown the cities!'

His motley audience seemed to have heard some of it before, and urged him on towards a crescendo of vision, a kind of angry, exultant chanting that I had never heard at any ordinary, decorous poetry reading, where the responses were often as subdued as in church. To me, it sounded like a redemptorist preacher cutting loose in a hellfire sermon, only the heavy stresses and long litanies were neither Anglo-Saxon nor Roman Catholic, but the sonorous cadences of the Hebraic tradition. Did I really hear phrases like 'Holy my mother in the insane asylum! Holy the cocks of the grandfathers of Kansas!'? Or lines celebrating the new San Francisco jazz scene: 'Holy the groaning saxophone! Holy the bop apocalypse! Holy the jazzbands marijuana hipsters peace & junk & drums!'? The audience were with him all the way, shouting the poetic equivalent of 'Go, man, go.' I was astonished by the blend of prophecy and

CHAPTER NINE

humour, so wildly present in two other new poems by Allen from the same period, 'A Supermarket in California' and 'America', with its famous, defiant conclusion, 'America, I'm putting my queer shoulder to the wheel.'

I thought no one could follow such a poetic upheaval, but as Allen settled back into his quiet student self, a trim bearded figure took over, reading poems about logging and climbing in the Pacific Northwest.

> Each dawn is clear
> Cold air bites the throat.
> Thick frost on the pine bough
> Leaps from the tree
>   snapped by the diesel

They were the first poems I had heard about physical labour, ordinary work, since I had left Ireland, and their quiet mysticism, as compared to the wilder shores of Ginsberg, reminded me of the best of Kavanagh. It was Gary Snyder, just about to return to a Zen monastery in Japan. When I would return to Berkeley, almost a decade later, he would be one of my closest companions.

After this foreshadowing of my future life in Berkeley, I folded back on myself, absorbed with seminars and correcting clumsy student essays. Tom was a fine, cantankerous teacher, trying to get the students to wake up, to think for themselves, if necessary by using shock tactics. One day, finding them docile as sheep, he ordered them to rise to their feet and stand by the windows.

'Now jump out,' he snorted with satisfaction.

In the whole class, I was the only one who laughed: even in sunny California, American students were still obedient and torpid as sleepwalkers, despite that fiery poetry reading, and films like *Rebel Without a Cause*.

I hitch-hiked along Route 66 to more exotic places, like D.H. Lawrence's Taos and Santa Fe, to meet Madeleine for Thanksgiving. She set out for Berkeley for Christmas, but her train got stuck in the Mojave desert, when the rains came. I describe my turmoil in a poem called 'All Legendary Obstacles':

> All day I waited, shifting
> Nervously from station to bar
> As I saw another train sail
> By, the San Francisco Chief or
> Golden Gate, water dripping
> From great flanged wheels.

When she finally arrived, I proposed to her, and we began to plan our common future, which included writing a formal request for her hand, in my stilted French, to her old-fashioned, aristocratic parents in Normandy.

We met again in Denver at Easter, and then Parkinson arranged that I taught a Summer Session, when Madeleine, released from her own duties, would be able to join me in Berkeley. It was a splendid summer: in the afternoons we played tennis in the Rose Garden, overlooking the glimmering Bay. And in the evenings we took the F train to San Francisco, eating at the Little Pisa on North Beach, or wandering along Fisherman's Wharf. At night there were the old-fashioned bump and grind joints of the International Settlement, and sometimes one of the more sophisticated jazz night clubs like the Black Hawk, only beginning to be known. Europeans like Madeleine and myself were exotic then, and we met a lot of curiosity and friendliness. Did I really enter into conversation with a large, humorous, extremely gifted bass player called Charlie Mingus? I loved the alto sax of Paul Desmond, and chatted with the group's leader, the pianist Dave Brubeck, about going to Paris. 'Do you really think they'd like us over there?' he asked incredulously. From the raucous beat of the strip joints to the muted modern strains of the clubs, it was the best jazz I had ever heard, sounds that would not reach Europe until later, so we were privileged.

The Bay Area enticed like the Garden of Eden, but we both wanted to leave it, to go back to make our home in Europe, which somehow seemed more real. Parkinson was disappointed, and said he would get me another scholarship, but I was adamant, and since he had spent a year in Bordeaux, and planned to work on the Yeats manuscripts in Dublin, he was reluctantly sympathetic to our plans. Besides, it was becoming obvious that I was a bit too wayward to be an ideal Berkeley PhD student, with back-to-back unbroken straight A's, like my friend Don Fanger, who would become the Professor of Slavic Languages at Harvard. A mimeographed copy of *Howl* rested on my desk, and a stream of visitors, French and English, including Malcolm Bradbury whom Madeleine had met in the Midwest, picked it up, intrigued and puzzled, but mainly condemnatory. Although nearly all the elements were there, it was still early days in the San Francisco poetry renaissance, and we were not yet accustomed to the idea of being '... fucked in the ass by saintly motorcyclists ...' I tried to crystallise the ambiguities of my situation in a series of sonnets about my exiled Jesuit uncle in Australia.

The Pacific waves crash in upon the beach,

> Roll and rise and inward stretch upon the beach.
> It is December now and warm…
> … In a dream
> I hear the cuckoo dance his double notes,
> Among the harvest stooks like golden chessmen;
> Each call an age, a continent between.

As a putative future father and family man, I needed a job, so I wrote to my old Professor of English at UCD, but he brusquely told me that there were no prospects and I seemed to be doing very well where I was. But Roger McHugh, who was developing a department in Anglo-Irish literature, was more understanding, and found me a job in, of all places, the Irish Tourist Board. I began to write to my family, to prepare them for my marriage, and the long voyage home.

II
Return to Paradise

'Here they are,' said a wry Madeleine recently, handing me a bulky manila envelope with 1958–1968 scrawled on it, 'the letters you wrote me over a decade. It was not wise to leave you so much alone. I have told that to my stepdaughter who wants to marry a boy who lives in Germany. Long separations are not good for a marriage. Too far away, you drift apart …'

*

I returned to Berkeley in 1964, again at the behest of Tom Parkinson. I have described how Tom came to Dublin to work on the Yeats manuscripts, and introduced me to Mrs Yeats, whom he admired for

CHAPTER NINE

her patience and her pungent perceptions about people, including her late husband. And I would meet Tom and his artist wife, Ariel – as short as he was tall – in England where he was teaching at York University; we walked the walls and visited the Shambles when I was on my way to read at Morden Tower. And he came to visit us in Paris, etcetera, in all the weaving patterns of a long-distance friendship. He was sceptically interested in the long poem I was working on, but felt I should read more contemporary American, especially West Coast, poetry, to get a more fluid and flexible line.

But I did not have any real intention of returning to Berkeley, fascinated as I was by the layers of French life, the drama of the Algerian confrontation, and the intense Parisian literary world I was striving to be a part of. Then something happened which tilted the balance, something that was part of the dark side of America, which we had glimpsed hitch-hiking through the remote south, as well as in the great urban centres like the Watts district of Los Angeles. Tom had been a maverick in his youth, running with a generation of poets with radical convictions in both politics and sex; Robert Duncan was a kind of alter ego for him, a wall-eyed homosexual bard devoted to the esoteric, a student of Blake and Yeats.

But of course always in the U.S., especially in California, the right-wing element rages underneath the surface. One morning, a local fanatic climbed into the Berkeley hills with his shotgun, where he spent several hours brooding on how he could rout the conspiracy of evil which he was convinced had infested the campus. He prepared a list of the major suspects, 'commies' and 'homos', and came down to clean out the lot. The first on his list was not in his office, but Parkinson was, when the intruder burst in. Although his size should have made Tom an easy target, the fanatic partly missed him, blowing off his lower jaw, but killing the graduate student who was his Teaching Assistant, the same post I had held some years earlier.

I tried to keep Tom's spirits up through correspondence, and I gathered that some of his colleagues had been less than kind, speculating spitefully that the gunman might have been a disaffected ex-lover from the San Francisco gay underworld. So when he pressed me to come back to Berkeley for the spring term of 1964, I could hardly refuse. Besides, I had completed my first book of stories, *Death of a Chieftain*, and was gathering a book of poems, a sequel to *Poisoned Lands*. I needed the kick start of change, but in the event, perhaps I got more than I had bargained for.

I flew back to California via New York, where I gave my first poetry reading at the 92nd Street Y, already the most venerable venue in the English-speaking world. I was reading with my friend Desmond O'Grady, our poetic man in Rome, and we met for the ritual few drinks the night before, in the White Horse Tavern, together with Jose Garcia Villa, an exclamatory bard beloved of Edith Sitwell.

I loved the variety and diversity of the city where I had been born, much more than when I was at Yale in the Cold War 1950s, with Joe McCarthy stalking the commies, and Dylan Thomas trying to kill himself in the very bar where we now celebrated his memory. My hostess in the Dakota, for instance, was an extraordinary lady called Bananas O'Rourke, a former student of Parkinson's who had come into a lot of money, and was not quite sure what to do with it. She maintained afterwards that throwing a pre-reading party for myself and Desmond launched her on a career as a literary hostess, becoming the Lady Ottoline Morrell of the Upper West Side, with a distinguished list of lovers. I liked Bananas, who was basically a simple, kind girl burdened with too much money, which attracts

CHAPTER NINE

predators. She had a daughter, and we used to wheel her to the lake in Central Park, simple pleasures which her husband did not seem capable of, his favourite sport being to throw the baby in the air when he came back from the bar. Bananas and her small daughter rattled like two peas in the enormous, sombre rooms of that extraordinary apartment house.

I also met two very different poets, who illustrated the extraordinary range of American poetry at that time. Patric Farrell, famous for being an Irishman who had never been in Ireland, brought me across the Brooklyn Bridge, near where I had been born, to the home of Marianne Moore, a book-laden room where she lived like an elegant bird in its nest. She reminded me of one of the more austere and affectionate of my Montague spinster aunts, and we exchanged books with the ritual courtesy of real writers, which overwhelmed me so much that I hardly spoke on the way back, Patric striding before me with his blackthorn and black hat like some legendary figure from the Irish past.

James Dickey was also in town, reading after us at the Y. He was at the height of his form, intoning the poems from *Buckdancer's Choice* with the mellifluous charm of a snake-oil salesman, and he did charm the crowd at a big party in his honour on the Upper East Side. I saw him cast a spell over a timid young girl, over whom he leaned and loomed like a boa constrictor before a rabbit, wrapping her round in the coils of his warm, so-southern voice. She had probably heard him read the raunchy love scene in 'Cherrylog Road', where '...the blacksnake, stiff / With inaction, curved back / Into life, and hunted the mouse'. He reminded me of the country boys of my Tyrone youth, the original red-necks, and his rough charm enchanted me as well, as we both sipped our amber, fiery Jack Daniels. It seemed to me that there was something marvellous about the many voices of American poetry, just as I had been delighted by the diversity of the city of my birth.

*

And now I was flying again to San Francisco; air travel made my bi-located 1960s possible, indeed exhilarating. Leave-takings were less wrenching: I had grown up with the legacy of the American Wake, family members journeying to the States perhaps forever, but I would fly back to Europe from California in a day. Flying was still a great adventure and planes were far more glamorous in the early 1960s than they are in this age of package tours and charter flights, with planes crowded and cramped, the Greyhound buses of the sky. A sweet, trim air hostess brought a United Air Lines biro to my window seat so that I could write Madeleine as the plane approached San Francisco:

'The journey out was superb. The Midwest lying under snow with the Platte River winding down below, and then the barrier of the Rockies. All a kind of giant chequerboard, with a city like Laramie only a pattern of lights. We were flying at about 30,000 feet, so the mountains looked artificially small; like a large classroom relief map. One begins to understand the elation of the astronauts, as they saw the world spread out beneath them. When you come out, you must try to fly across the western part of the United States in the daytime.'

And I was delighted to be bringing home some of the bacon again. Another comment, intended as a humorous boast, betrays my uneasiness about my position as kept man in Paris: 'At long last you are married to a serious man, with a stake in society, whom people call Doctor over the telephone. Only an occasional tremor of the

CHAPTER NINE

voice, or twitch of the eyelid, reveals that he is not quite sure what he is doing here at all.' I was not merely proud of my renewed status as wage-earner, but also to be back in the Academy, only on the other side of the desk as, writing on English Department stationery, I exult, 'What sumptuous note paper. I can't resist it!'

I was also re-discovering a landscape I had loved, and wrote of walking down to the Rose Garden: 'The weather has been wonderful. The evenings have alternate wafts of heat and coolness. And then the city – the whole Bay Area shining like a vast lily pond, with little points of light where the cars flow on the freeway, and occasional red lights in the sky, from small planes coming in to land. An extraordinary lambent vision of man's enterprise …' Elsewhere I noted, 'I feel my European self dissolve, and feel I should take another name, like Sourdough John or Monterey Jack, the best local cheese, by the way.'

Weekends I wandered over to San Francisco with big Tom, for some mild R&R. He was friendly with a brilliant student who would later become a well-known feminist scholar and critic, and tired of playing Gooseberry, I began a light affair with her flatmate, a sweet, plump young woman from southern California, who was earning her living as an apprentice belly dancer. She brought some of her professional skills to the bed, which was very pleasant. But when she began to systematically plunder the Kama Sutra by her bedside, researching new and more elaborate positions, I felt I had to call a halt, especially as I was exhausted after a week's teaching in Berkeley, not an easy billet. 'Can't we just make love?' I cried wearily. She was astonished, because she had never thought of it in such a simple manner, being used to sex as a point-scoring exercise on the trampoline, technique as opposed to tenderness.

That was my first practical attempt at an extra-marital affair, to ease my physical needs while ignoring my real and growing loneliness, trying to conduct a dalliance like a real Frenchman. We broke up, laughing, and apart from another half-hearted attempt to establish a friendship with a black nurse, I tried to content myself with my quite draining work at the University – my post at Berkeley was no sinecure – and getting to know my colleagues. An extraordinary lady, Josephine Miles, conducted a full life as professor, poet and critic despite being disabled, ferried by graduate students to her various classes. A fine poet, Louis Simpson, was down the corridor, and we shared our unease about aspects of this New World we found ourselves in; his poetic report on the subject, *At the End of the Open Road*, won the Pulitzer prize for poetry that year. Although the book disparaged California, Simpson was toasted with champagne in the English Department, even by Patriot Parkinson. Thom Gunn was also around, discreetly dressed as the rest of us, except for his tell-tale cowboy boots. We did not fraternise much in the department, but met now and again on the F (no longer train but bus) to San Francisco.

With her usual aplomb, Madeleine came and went by helicopter from Oakland; she had arranged to come to an economic conference in Washington. Her brief visit soothed me, but after she left my loneliness returned in force: 'The world seems to mourn your absence. San Francisco and the Bay are obscured in a damp fog ... as I write the clouds are quite perceptibly lifting, as though the thought of you cheered them. And Angel Island appears, and the water of the bay: Hurrah!' But although she herself had tutored me in the French style of marriage, where affairs were considered a natural way of letting off steam, and might even be good for the couple, my deep need for steadiness emerged in the same letter: 'I feel much less restless, certainly, than before you came, as though

CHAPTER NINE

your brief stay had reminded me of who I am, and where we both stand (immutably) and how my present world joins our past.' Obviously I did not have the temperament for the kind of schematic love life prevailing in France from *Les Liaisons Dangereuses* to the complicated arrangements of Jean-Paul and Simone.

Swimming in the men's gymnasium, picnicking in the sunlit Berkeley hills, I diverted myself as best I could. Mary McCarthy came out from the East; I lent her my office, and enjoyed her company, although I was made uneasy by something of the same earnest intensity that I had felt in Doris Lessing, the programmatic fervour of the *Partisan Review* or *New Statesman* crowd. And she did not endear herself to me by denying her Irishness. Eugene O'Neill 'could not write', she pronounced, flashing her automatic smile across the dinner table.

She delivered a series of rather patronising lectures on Shakespeare and the Conspiracy Theory of History, especially relevant after the JFK assassination. She maintained that Americans (especially in sunny, mindless California) were too naïve to understand that conspiracy was inevitably a part of political life, as Europeans – and New Yorkers by extension – had always known. Of course Tom 'Redwood' Parkinson was boiling: people coming to California to lecture the Natives on their lack of sophistication aroused his especial wrath, since he thought that Northern California, with its vines, its balmy climate and its abundance of poets, could well be considered the most civilised part of the country.

*

Then something happened which shook me to the foundations. I drifted into a love affair with a younger colleague which turned immediately serious, too serious. She was at the end of her first year in Berkeley, and engaged to be married to someone in Europe, so she had been a long time alone. And I was also coming to the end of my first stint as a professor at Berkeley, and girding my loins for the return; my letters to Paris echoed with loneliness. But instead of ferrying our respective yearnings home, we plunged into a sensual maelstrom fuelled by long abstinence and absence. Besides, I was a poet in my mid-thirties, and she was an exotic-looking young woman with a husky voice, evoking, in my all-too-dreamy, literary mind, Shakespeare's dark lady: 'If hair be wires, black wires grow on her head.' In 'A Charm' I acknowledge her spell:

> When you step near
> I feel the dark hood
> Descend, a shadow
> Upon my mind.

Her sexual intensity, which seemed in keeping with her dark mysterious looks, took me by surprise, especially since, after so long in France, I thought I knew everything about *amour*, the art of love. But some people are so refined by their obsessions that they become almost archetypes, a single burning quality, the heat of lust or the erotic girdle of Aphrodite. This young woman, with her sexual audacity and nearly inexhaustible appetite, seemed an embodiment of some primal force, Kali or Coatlicue, which both intrigued and frightened me. In fact, I would compare her to the Mexican goddess in 'Coatlicue':

> Black hair swings
> over your shoulders

CHAPTER NINE

> as you bear darkness
> down towards me...

I broke away to explore the Pacific Northwest, calling on Jim Dickey at Reed College, where we watched a green sliding river and sang together: Jim improvised a song, 'Poisoned lands where I did dwell / Before I sang my way to hell ... ' It seemed vaguely prophetic, and I told him and Carolyn Kizer the Sweeney legend, which had always haunted me, the image of the poet-king who becomes almost a bird. Carolyn brought me to the Portland and Seattle museums, my first glimpse of the powerful art of the Pacific Coast Indians, which filtered through into the contemporary work of Mark Tobey and my friend Morris Graves, whose house outside Dublin, Woodtown Manor, I adored for its balance of the inner and outer worlds. I read under her auspices at Seattle, and, at a big party afterwards, met Ted Roethke's still-mourning widow, a striking figure with a chalk-white face and long dark hair which suited her Romantic name, Beatrice.

My now exiled Yorkshire friend, Robin Skelton, met me in Vancouver for a Canadian radio broadcast, and I travelled with him by ferry to Vancouver Island, another site for powerful North American Indian art, giant totem poles rising incongruously near the old-fashioned Empress Hotel. We got drunk in that marvellously Victorian setting, so drunk that by accident I gave our driver a fifty-dollar tip in the semi-darkness of the taxi on our return home. I found the Pacific Northwest, with its soaring mountains and clear cold rivers, a kind of giant Ireland, and I vowed to return, all the more because I felt at ease with the local poets, including Gary Snyder, who had just come back again from his Buddhist studies in Japan. He and Jack Kerouac had been forest look-outs in these same mountains.

Gary gave a series of splendid, controlled readings on the Berkeley campus, first in Parkinson's class, then a large public reading where academics mingled with those bearded mystics, garbed like old-style frontiersmen, who would later be called hippies: Gary was already a guru for a new generation. Some new energy was cresting, and I allowed myself to be cajoled by the head of the English Department, a quiet-spoken American scholar called Henry Nash Smith, to return to Berkeley the following spring. In the meantime I was preparing to return to Paris, still missing Madeleine and my French life, but confused by what had happened. There was a bumper poetry reading at San Francisco State, as a round-up to the academic year. I stayed with an old Iowa workshop pal, Bill Dickey, and he was sympathetic to my strained state, which became obvious to everyone as I stumbled through my reading. The other Dickey, the ebullient Jim, had read before me, and wowed the audience with an extraordinary new poem called 'The Shark's Parlour', full of the blood and guts beloved of the hunter. All I could say as an apology for my wounded state was that I seemed to be demonstrating the state of mind of the hunted, after hearing Big Jim reeling out lines like:

> The shark flopped on the porch, grating with salt-sand
>   driving back in
> The nails he had pulled out
> Coughing chunks of his formless blood.
> The screen door banged and tore off
> He scrambled on his tail...

Then I took an Air France charter flight back to Paris, a long haul from San Francisco, broken by several splendid meals, which had

CHAPTER NINE

me walking up and down the plane, discreetly breaking wind. It seemed to me the plane leaped forward every time I farted, a Chaucerian fantasy spirited to the modern age. But my heart was heavy, and when I saw Madeleine's eager face, brown as a berry, at Orly airport, I did not know what to think, or what I had done.